# TACTICS AND STRATEGIES FOR AIRCRAFT FIREFIGHTING

# TACTICS AND STRATEGIES FOR AIRCRAFT FIREFIGHTING

# TACTICS AND STRATEGIES FOR AIRCRAFT FIREFIGHTING

**Author**:

Andrés Felipe Rendón López

**Cover design and illustration**:

Vanessa Gomez

**Legal deposit**:

ISB: 9798300689155

**Copyright © October 2024**

Emerti S.A.S

All rights reserved.

**Printing:**

Aguirre printers

Cellular 3175697775

# TACTICS AND STRATEGIES FOR AIRCRAFT FIREFIGHTING

## TABLE OF CONTENTS

### ☐ Introduction

### ☐ Chapter 1: Airport Analysis

### ☐ Chapter 2: Response Planning

## ☐ Chapter **3: Implementing the Action Plan**

## ☐ Chapter **4: Evaluating Progress**

## ☐ Chapter **5: Ending the Incident**

# TACTICS AND STRATEGIES FOR AIRCRAFT FIREFIGHTING

# DEDICATION

I dedicate this book to my family for their patience, their constant support, their encouragement, to my wife especially for being there from the first day I decided to become an Aeronautical Firefighter, to my children because in their childhood I had to be away for a long time, training new Firefighters and in spite of everything they are good people from whom I have always received only support and words of encouragement.

To my co-workers from my first airport "Almirante Padilla" in Riohacha, from there began the basis to become what I am, to learn to be disciplined and to learn to love what I do since September 1, 1999.

To my co-workers at the "Eldorado" Airport in Bogota from 2002 to 2004, the tenacity of each one, the experience that should not be overlooked, taught me to be strong, to fight to change things for the better, to know that there is always a black and white, a yin and a yang, that what we have to look for is balance.

To my coworkers at the "Alfonso Bonilla Aragón" Airport in Cali, my home since 2004 and where I currently live, my brothers for exactly 20 years now, I dedicate this book to you for being my support, for helping me to change history, for standing out, even if we stir the dust, for not keeping quiet.

To CEA, my alma mater, thank you for hosting me for more than 21 years as a teacher, for believing in me, for giving me such great responsibilities as being an ICAO training trainer and for being able to write important works on your behalf that are now in the TPEMS library.

## TACTICS AND STRATEGIES FOR AIRCRAFT FIREFIGHTING

## Andrés Felipe Rendón López

Born in Cali (Valle del Cauca) COLOMBIA in 1979 but established his residence in Yumbo (Valle del Cauca) more than 20 years ago.

He began his career in emergency response in the Colombian Civil Defense, Jamundí (Valle del Cauca), then in the year 1.995 becomes part of the ranks of the Meritorious Volunteer Fire Department of Jamundí, in parallel began his studies as a Medical Emergency Technician at the Hospital Universitario del Valle in Cali with the Corporation special rescue group, works for the University of Valle directing the laboratory skills and abilities in health until 1.998, is formed as Aeronautical Firefighter in the Center for Aeronautical Studies in 1.999 and began his career in this field in the same year in Riohacha (La Guajira), there, he joined the Colombian Red Cross Guajira departmental section where he served until 2002 as Instructor, departmental coordinator of the specialties of aquatic rescue and pre-hospital care, in the year 2.002 is transferred to the city of Bogota, to the International Airport "Eldorado" and serves as national training coordinator for Aircraft Rescue Firefighters in the Center for Aeronautical Studies CEA (to date) is currently an instructor trainer for the ICAO, in 2002.In 2004 he was transferred to Cali, to the International Airport "Alfonso Bonilla Aragón" where he remains until the present, in 2004 he joined the ranks of the Benemérito

## TACTICS AND STRATEGIES FOR AIRCRAFT FIREFIGHTING

Cuerpo de Bomberos Voluntarios de Yumbo (Valle del Cauca) where he remains until the year 2.013.


He has dedicated his life to the training of new firefighters inside and outside the country (Mexico, Panama, United States, Ecuador, Venezuela, Bolivia, Chile) and to date continues to serve as an instructor in different specialties.

## About this book

Aircraft firefighting is one of the greatest challenges faced by Aircraft Rescue Firefighters. The unique characteristics of incidents involving aircraft, coupled with the strict regulations and inherent urgency of these situations, require meticulous preparation based on effective tactics and sound operational strategies. This book, **"Tactics and Strategies for Aircraft Firefighting,"** is designed to provide a comprehensive and practical approach for Aircraft Rescue Firefighters, offering complete guidance on how to deal with the

various types of incidents that can occur at airports, from analysis to resolution of the event.

To see the introduction to the book, scan the QR code.

Each chapter has been developed with the objective of guiding the reader through the decision-making process and operational actions, aligned with international best practices and the most updated regulations. The references used, such as **NFPA** standards, ICAO documents, FAA circulars, ICAO Standardized Training Packages (STP), provide the necessary theoretical and practical frameworks to face aeronautical emergencies, while the author's experience, with more than 26 years as an aeronautical firefighter and 21 years as an Aeronautical Firefighter instructor, ensures that the content is applicable to the operational reality of firefighters in airports around the world.

This book is based on the APIET (Analysis, Planning, Implementation, Evaluation and Termination) process, an approach widely used in emergency management, including situations involving aircraft. This process is fundamental to ensure an efficient and organized response to critical situations, allowing constant evaluation and adjustments according to the evolution of events.

## TACTICS AND STRATEGIES FOR AIRCRAFT FIREFIGHTING

**Analysis:** In this first phase, risks and available resources are assessed. In the case of aircraft emergencies, the analysis includes the identification of hazards such as fuel fires, compromised structures, and proximity to sensitive areas. The National Fire Protection Association (NFPA) standard NFPA 403 provides specific guidelines on the minimum requirements for Aircraft Rescue and Fire Fighting Services (ARFF) at airports, which is key during this initial phase for sizing the necessary rescue and extinguishing resources.

In **Chapter 1: Analysis of Potential Incidents/Accidents**, we addressed the importance of familiarity with the airport environment and aircraft, critical elements for a quick and efficient response. Topics such as **grid maps** and identification of **rapid access and critical access areas** (NFPA 402, 2022; FAA, 2022) are fundamental to understanding the structure and critical points of airports and aircraft. Without this knowledge, ARFF teams cannot optimize their response time or properly position their resources (ICAO, 2023), and it is vitally important to know that good planning depends on analysis.

**2. Planning:** Once the scenario and resources are identified, actions are planned. Coordination between ARFF teams, medical teams and other emergency services is vital. NFPA 424 provides guidance for community and airport emergency planning, highlighting the importance of plans that include predefined procedures and regular drills to prepare personnel for aircraft accidents.

**Chapter 2: Response Planning** introduces the reader to the **Incident Command System (ICS)**, a key tool for organizing response teams during any aviation emergency (USAID BHA OFDA, 2020). This chapter explains how to develop an **Incident Action Plan (IAP)**, establish **command levels, standby levels, the scheme of work of 3,** and leads to organize teams under an efficient scheme of work. In addition, it emphasizes the value of **headcount,**

a vital aspect of ensuring firefighter safety during operations (NFPA 403, 2022).

**3. Implementation:** In this phase, the designed actions are carried out. In the context of aircraft emergencies, implementation involves the rapid intervention of the ARFF to control fires, ensure the safe evacuation of passengers, and stabilize the accident area. The NFPA 403 standard establishes specific response times for ARFF teams, with the objective of minimizing human and material losses.

**Chapter 3: Implementing the Action Plan** details the **response sequence, tactical priorities**, and **exterior and interior securing** measures. Here, the reader will learn how to execute the action plan based on the type of incident, maximizing efficiency in rescue and firefighting operations (CEA, 2023). In addition, specific techniques are described to contain fires and ensure the safety of the aircraft occupants, following the standards defined by **NFPA** and **ICAO**.

**4. Evaluation:** During and after the emergency, the performance of the implemented actions is evaluated. This step is crucial to identify failures or areas for improvement. NFPA also highlights the need for post-incident reviews to learn from each situation and adjust future procedures, which is part of the standard for continuous improvement in emergency management.

In **Chapter 4: Evaluating Progress**, we use the **Deming Cycle** as a tool for continuous improvement during the operation, allowing personnel to adjust their tactics as the incident evolves (IFSTA, 2023). **Objective evaluation** ensures that decisions are made based on data, allowing for greater accuracy in execution and avoiding errors that could compromise the operation (SRVSOP, 2017).

**5. Termination:** Finally, the operation is concluded, ensuring that all risks have been controlled and the site is in a safe condition. Termination procedures include the safe removal of personnel and the restoration of normal operations at the airport, according to established safety guidelines.

Finally, **Chapter 5: Ending the Incident** addresses the crucial phase of **demobilization, operational** and **administrative closure,** and **final debriefing.** These steps are essential to ensure that all resources are safely removed and that teams are prepared for the next emergency (NFPA 1003, 2022). In addition, post-incident analysis allows for the implementation of improvements in operating procedures for future emergencies (USAID BHA OFDA, 2020), and the reestablishment of rescue and firefighting service on Aircraft.

**APIET** becomes a robust model when integrated with NFPA regulations, as it ensures that actions are efficient, aligned with international best practices and tailored to the specific characteristics of aircraft emergencies.

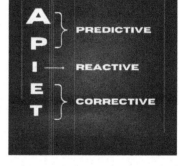

Throughout this book, the reader will find not only the necessary tactics to deal with aircraft emergencies, but also a clear and sequential structure to address each stage of the incident. From the initial analysis to the final closure, this book becomes an indispensable tool for any aeronautical firefighter who wishes to improve his operational and tactical capabilities in aircraft firefighting.

## References

NFPA. (2018). NFPA 403: Standard for Aircraft Rescue and Fire-Fighting Services at Airports.

NFPA. (2024). NFPA 424: Guide for Airport/Community Emergency Planning.

# CHAPTER 1

# ANALYSIS OF POSSIBLE INCIDENTS/ACCIDENTS

# TACTICS AND STRATEGIES FOR AIRCRAFT FIREFIGHTING

## INTRODUCTION

The analysis of potential incidents and accidents is the critical first step in any aeronautical firefighting response operation. A thorough understanding of the different scenarios that may present themselves during an aircraft emergency is essential to plan effectively and avoid unforeseen situations. As aircraft firefighting experts, it is imperative that Aircraft Rescue Firefighters understand all the factors involved in a potential incident, from the configuration of the airport to the specific characteristics of the aircraft involved.

This chapter addresses the fundamentals of incident and accident analysis, with a focus on familiarization with the operational environment. This includes the study of airport grid maps (ICAO, 2023), understanding the areas of rapid access and critical areas, and identifying the resources needed for the task of rescue and firefighting (NFPA 403, 2022). This analysis allows establishing the basis for detailed planning, ensuring that each team is prepared for any eventuality.

The importance of this analysis lies in the need to gather essential data to avoid surprises at the time of the emergency. Aircraft fires are characterized by their speed and volatility, which requires that response teams not only have adequate resources, but also be strategically positioned to act quickly. According to NFPA 402 (2022), prior knowledge of access routes, resource readiness, and response times is key to reducing the impact of an incident.

In addition, aircraft familiarization is a vital component of the analysis. Firefighters must be aware of access points, fuel tank locations, and structural features that could influence fire behavior (ICAO, 2023). This knowledge is critical to tailor extinguishing and rescue tactics to each aircraft type, ensuring a more effective and safer response.

## TACTICS AND STRATEGIES FOR AIRCRAFT FIREFIGHTING

In aviation nothing can be left to chance, that is why everything is planned, I invite you to scan the QR code and watch the video to calculate the theoretical and practical critical areas, as well as the amounts of water needed to form foam to control and suppress fires in the practical critical area in 1 minute.

Detailed analysis of these factors not only contributes to better planning, but also prepares teams to adjust to changing realities during the incident. Poor planning or lack of accurate information can lead to improvisation during the operation, which increases the risk of response failure. As the CRESIA Alumni Handbook (CEA, 2023) aptly states, "success in emergency response is directly dependent on advance preparation and the ability to anticipate challenges that may arise."

In summary, this chapter provides the necessary tools for Aircraft Rescue Firefighters to carry out an exhaustive analysis of the possible incidents or accidents that may occur, which is essential for developing a good response action plan.

# TACTICS AND STRATEGIES FOR AIRCRAFT FIREFIGHTING

## 1.1 Airport Analysis

### 1.1.1 Knowledge of Bridge and Ramp Loading Capacities at Airports

Airport infrastructure plays a fundamental role in the safety and effectiveness of emergency operations, especially in aircraft firefighting. The load capacity of bridges and ramps at airports is a critical aspect that must be understood and evaluated by aeronautical firefighting teams. This knowledge not only affects the logistics of access to the aircraft in case of emergency, but also influences the response strategy in critical situations.

Bridges and ramps must be designed to withstand significant loads, considering the weight of emergency vehicles, rescue equipment and materials to be used during an intervention. According to the **National Fire Protection Association (NFPA)**, regulations require that structures at airports be capable of withstanding dynamic and static loads encountered during rescue operations (NFPA 409, 2020). This includes the evaluation of firefighting vehicles, which can weigh between 10 and 40 tons, depending on their configuration and equipment.

The **International Civil Aviation Organization (ICAO)** also sets standards for airport infrastructure, stressing the importance of load-carrying capacity on access roads and operating areas (ICAO Annex 14, 2019). These standards ensure that, in the event of a fire or accident, Aircraft Rescue Firefighters have immediate and safe access to the aircraft and any casualties at the scene.

### Success Stories in Real Emergencies

One notable case, which highlights the importance of understanding airport cargo capacity, is the fire that occurred at Miami International Airport in 2016. In this incident, an airliner suffered a fire in the engine area during the deplaning run. Thanks to the robust design of the airport's ramps and bridges, fire trucks were able to quickly access the incident site, allowing for an agile response that resulted in the successful evacuation of all passengers and extinguishment of the fire in record time. Post-incident reports indicated that prior knowledge of the loading capacity of the ramps allowed firefighters to optimize their movements and ensure that heavy vehicles did not get stuck around operations.

Another significant example is the United Airlines Flight 93 incident in 2001, where Aircraft Rescue Firefighters faced the challenge of accessing unprepared terrain due to the crash of the aircraft in a rural area. Although this was not an airport, the principles of load carrying capacity and access planning were similarly applied. The firefighters had to use specific equipment that allowed them to access difficult terrain, emphasizing the importance of considering the load capacity and suitability of the equipment in each situation.

### 1.1.2 Rapid Access Areas and Critical Access Areas

Airport planning and design not only focus on aircraft operational efficiency, but must also consider accessibility for emergency crews, especially Aircraft Rescue Firefighters. In this context, rapid access areas and critical access areas are essential components that must be thoroughly understood and analyzed by emergency responders. This section will address the **National Fire Protection Association (NFPA)** standards, as well as the practical strategies derived from these standards and their application in real situations.

### Importance of Quick Access Areas

Rapid access areas, according to NFPA, are those that allow emergency vehicles to reach an aircraft in optimum time. **NFPA 409**, in its section on emergency response operations, states that airports should have designated areas that facilitate immediate access to aircraft, minimizing response time and ensuring that the appropriate 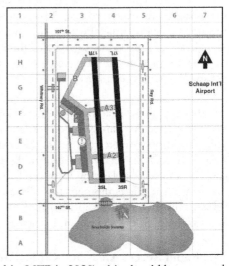 equipment is readily available (NFPA, 2020), this should be captured on a grid map, and Firefighters should be thoroughly familiar with them and with the day-to-day changes in the areas of influence.

This rapid accessibility is crucial in situations where every second counts. A notable example is the American Airlines Flight 11 fire at Boston International Airport in 2001. Thanks to the designation of rapid access areas, fire crews were able to reach the scene of the incident in less than two minutes, allowing the fire to be contained and passengers to be evacuated without additional loss of life (FAA, 2002).

### Critical Access Areas

Critical access areas are those that require special attention, as they are strategically important for the safety of airport operations. These areas include not only areas around runways and gates, but also service areas where maintenance and fueling activities are carried out.

## TACTICS AND STRATEGIES FOR AIRCRAFT FIREFIGHTING

According to **International Civil Aviation Organization (ICAO)** regulations, critical access areas must be clearly identified and clear of obstructions to ensure that emergency vehicles can maneuver smoothly. This is complemented by NFPA, which requires critical access areas to be adequately signposted and have sufficient lighting (ICAO Annex 14, 2019).

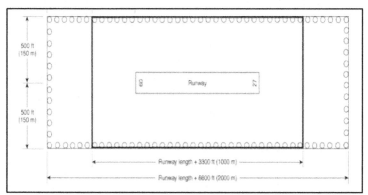

A successful case of utilizing critical access areas was observed in a crash-landing incident at San Francisco Airport in 2013. During this event, the aircraft that suffered a technical failure landed off the runway. Quick identification and access to critical areas allowed firefighters to perform an efficient assessment and response, bringing the fire under control within minutes and ensuring the safety of all involved.

### Strategies to Optimize Access

Planning for rapid and critical access areas should include several strategies to optimize emergency response. These strategies may include:

1. **Efficient Infrastructure Design**: Airports should be designed to include direct access routes to critical and high activity areas. This includes the removal of obstacles that may delay the arrival of emergency vehicles.

2.  **Drills and Training**: Ongoing training and conducting emergency drills in collaboration with airport authorities are critical. These exercises allow response teams to familiarize themselves with the environment and the potential challenges they may face during an emergency.
3.  **Clear Signage**: Signage at the airport should be clear and visible, indicating quick access routes and critical areas. This will help firefighters quickly orient themselves and avoid confusion during high-pressure situations.
4.  **Effective Communication**: An efficient communication system between air traffic controllers and emergency crews is vital. This will ensure that accurate information about the location of incidents is transmitted and that firefighters have a clear understanding of the situation.

### 1.1.3 Types of Structures and their Fire Resistance

Understanding the different types of structures at an airport and their resistance to fire is crucial for Aircraft Rescue Firefighters. This knowledge not only facilitates the planning of firefighting strategies, but also allows for a more effective response in emergency situations. Airport structures, which include hangars, terminals, service buildings and control towers, present different challenges and characteristics that must be considered during fire intervention.

### Classification of Structures

Airport structures can be classified into several categories according to their function and design:

1.  **Hangars**: These are buildings designed to house aircraft. They usually have large open spaces and high ceilings, which can facilitate the accumulation of smoke and heat in case of fire. The fire resistance of hangars depends on the materials used in their construction. NFPA 409 states that hangars should be constructed of materials that meet certain fire resistance specifications (NFPA, 2020).

2.  **Passenger Terminals**: These structures are critical to
    airport operations and are generally designed to support
    large volumes of people. Their fire resistance is essential,
    since they may include combustible materials in areas such
    as stores and restaurants. **International Civil Aviation
    Organization (ICAO)** standards, stress the importance of
    using non-combustible materials in areas of high footfall
    (ICAO Annex 14, 2019).
3.  **Service Buildings**: These include maintenance and
    operations facilities that are critical to the operation of the
    airport. Their fire resistance must be evaluated to protect
    both personnel and critical equipment in case of fire.
4.  **Control Towers**: These structures are essential for air
    traffic management and must be designed to withstand fires
    that may occur in their vicinity. Safety in these areas is vital,
    as any disruption in tower operations can have serious
    consequences.

The evaluation of an airport's infrastructure must include the
different structures and their fire resistance, which are classified
according to NFPA standards into five main types:

- **Type I:** Non-combustible fire-resistant structures, with
  supports and walls constructed of steel or reinforced
  concrete. These structures offer the highest level of
  protection in case of fire.
- **Type II:** Non-combustible structures with a lower fire
  resistance than Type I structures. They have a similar
  design, but with less heat-resistant materials.
- **Type III:** Mixed structures with non-combustible exterior
  walls, but with interior elements of wood or other
  combustible materials.
- **Type IV:** Structures built with heavy timber and exposed
  connections. Although combustible, they offer greater
  resistance than type V due to the thickness of their
  components.

- **Type V:** Fully combustible structures, typically constructed of light wood.

| Type of Structure | Fire Resistance | Main Material | Airport Application |
|---|---|---|---|
| Type I | High | Steel/Reinforced Concrete | Main terminals |
| Type II | Media | Steel/Light Concrete | Aircraft hangar |
| Type III | Download | Wood and other fuels | Peripheral offices |
| Type IV | Media | Heavy Wood | Warehouses, small hangars |
| Type V | Very Low | Light Wood | Temporary structures |

This knowledge is vital, as it allows Aircraft Rescue Firefighters to tailor their tactics according to the fire resistance of each structure at the airport. At airports such as **Atlanta's Hartsfield-Jackson**, the terminals are mostly Type I and II, which facilitates longer containment time for firefighters before fire causes structural collapse.

## Importance of Fire Resistance

The fire resistance of these structures is determined by their ability to withstand extreme temperatures during a fire. According to NFPA, an adequate fire resistance rating is crucial to ensure that structures maintain their integrity for a given period, allowing occupants to evacuate safely and firefighters to conduct their operations without the risk of structural collapse (NFPA 5000, 2020).

## Success Stories in Real Emergencies

A notable example demonstrating the importance of fire resistance in airport structures occurred at Denver Airport in 2001. During an incident, an aircraft suffered a rear-end fire while in a hangar. Due to the adequate fire resistance of the hangar structure, the fire did not spread to surrounding areas, allowing firefighters to quickly contain the fire and ensure that no additional damage occurred. Reports indicated that the fire doors, which complied with NFPA regulations, played a crucial role in containing the fire (FAA, 2002).

Another successful case took place at Heathrow Airport, where a fire broke out in a passenger terminal. The structure, designed with non-combustible materials and smoke control systems, allowed for a rapid evacuation of passengers. Upon arrival at the scene, firefighting personnel were able to conduct their operations efficiently thanks to the terminal's fire resistance. This incident underscores the importance of construction and design standards in the prevention of major disasters.

## Strategies for Optimizing Fire Resistance

To ensure the effectiveness of fire resistance in airport structures, several strategies must be considered:

1. **Construction Materials**: Using non-combustible materials rated for fire resistance is critical. NFPA standards provide clear guidelines on the types of materials to be used in hangar and terminal construction.
2. **Regular Maintenance**: The implementation of maintenance programs to inspect and maintain structural integrity is essential. This includes periodic checks of fire

doors, fire detection and alarm systems, and fire
extinguishers.
3. **Training and Drills**: Response teams should participate in
fire drills that include specific scenarios related to airport
structures. This will allow firefighters to become familiar
with the characteristics of each type of structure and
practice their response.
4. **Response Planning**: Developing a response plan that
considers the structural characteristics and materials used in
each area of the airport is crucial to optimize operations in
the event of a fire.

### 1.1.4 Perimeter Roads

Perimeter roadways at an airport are a critical component of the
infrastructure that allows quick and efficient access to emergency
sites. These roadways are designed to facilitate the movement of
emergency vehicles, such as fire trucks and ambulances, to areas
where incidents may occur, which is vital to the safety and
management of emergency situations at the airport. This section will
discuss the importance of perimeter roadways in the operation of
Aircraft Rescue Firefighters, based on regulations from the
**National Fire Protection Association (NFPA)**, the
**International Civil Aviation Organization (ICAO)** and the
**Federal Aviation Administration (FAA)**.

### Importance of Perimeter Roads

Perimeter roads are essential for several reasons:

1. **Rapid Access**: These routes allow emergency crews to
reach any part of the airport in the shortest possible time.
According to NFPA, designated emergency response areas
should be clearly always marked and accessible (NFPA,
2020). This minimizes response time, which is crucial in
situations where every second counts.

2.  **Operational Safety**: Perimeter roads are essential to ensure
    safety at the airport, as they provide quick access not only
    to aircraft, but also to passengers and critical areas in the
    event of evacuations. This is particularly important during
    incidents involving passenger evacuation or fire control.
3.  **Resource Integration**: These lanes allow for the
    integration of different emergency resources and units,
    including fire, medical services, and police. Coordination of
    these resources is vital for effective emergency
    management, and perimeter roads facilitate this process.

## Relevant Regulations

The NFPA and ICAO establish clear guidelines for the planning and
design of perimeter roadways at airports. **NFPA 409** specifies that
the roadways must be designed to support the weight of emergency
vehicles and must be free of obstacles that could interrupt access
(NFPA, 2020). For its part, **ICAO** emphasizes the need to maintain
these roadways in optimal condition to ensure safe operations and
emergency response (ICAO Annex 14, 2019).

## Success Stories in Real Emergencies

One notable case that illustrates the importance of perimeter
walkways is an incident that occurred at Los Angeles International
Airport in 2016. During a fire on an airliner, firefighters were able to
quickly access the aircraft thanks to well-designed and maintained
perimeter lanes. This allowed for an efficient response time,
managing to evacuate passengers and bring the fire under control in
less than five minutes. Reports from this incident highlighted the
importance of having clear and well-marked access roads, which
facilitated the operation of emergency crews (FAA, 2017).

Another significant example occurred at Heathrow Airport in 2018,
where a smoke incident in the cabin of an aircraft required a rapid
response. Fire crews were able to reach the aircraft using the
perimeter tracks, allowing them to assess the situation and extinguish

any potential fire before it spread. The efficient management of this emergency highlighted how perimeter roads not only contribute to a faster response, but also help prevent major disasters.

### Strategies for the Optimization of Perimeter Roads

To maximize the effectiveness of perimeter roads, several strategies should be implemented:

1. **Adequate Design**: Roadways should be designed with sufficient width to allow for the passage of emergency vehicles, as well as the ability for multiple vehicles to pass each other without obstruction. NFPA recommends that the minimum track width be sufficient for the type of vehicles to be used (NFPA 409, 2020).
2. **Regular Maintenance**: Perimeter roads should be regularly maintained to ensure that they are free of debris and obstructions. This includes inspection of signage and repair of any damage to the track surface.
3. **Staff Training**: It is essential that emergency personnel are familiar with the layout and routing of perimeter roadways. Regular training and drills will help ensure that emergency crews can effectively navigate the airport.
4. **Clear Signage**: Roadways should be clearly marked to guide emergency vehicles to critical and quick-access areas. This will help reduce response time and minimize the risk of confusion during an emergency.

### 1.1.5 Difficult Sites

In the context of aircraft firefighting, the identification and understanding of difficult locations within an airport is crucial. These locations may include areas that are difficult to access, uneven terrain, and situations that present obstacles to rapid firefighter intervention. Planning and preparation for these challenges are essential to ensure the effectiveness of the emergency response and minimize the risk to human life and aircraft.

## TACTICS AND STRATEGIES FOR AIRCRAFT FIREFIGHTING

### Definition of Difficult Sites

Difficult locations at an airport can be defined as areas that, due to their location, design or environmental conditions, present difficulties for the mobilization of emergency equipment. Common examples include:

1. **Areas with Irregular Terrain**: These areas may be prone to flooding, mud, or rough terrain that makes it difficult for emergency vehicles to access.
2. **Areas Away from Main Roads**: Distance from perimeter roads can make certain points of the airport more difficult to reach in the event of an emergency. This is especially critical in situations where time is of the essence.
3. **Physical Obstructions**: The presence of obstructions such as buildings, utility equipment, and other structures may limit the movement of fire trucks and other emergency vehicles.

### Jungles

Jungles are one of the most complicated landscapes in the airport context. Characterized by dense vegetation, jungles can hinder aircraft access in emergency situations. The dense foliage and humidity can increase the risk of forest fires, further complicating the work of firefighters.

A significant example of an emergency in a jungle environment occurred at Manaus International Airport, Brazil, where a plane crashed in the surrounding jungle. Thanks to proper preparation and the use of off-road vehicles, rescue teams were able to quickly access the crash site and conduct search and rescue operations, saving several survivors (ANAC, 2017). This incident underscores the importance of having well-defined access routes and specific training to operate in this type of terrain.

# TACTICS AND STRATEGIES FOR AIRCRAFT FIREFIGHTING

## Deserts

Deserts, while they may seem less complex than jungles, present their own challenges. High temperatures, scarce water and loose sand can make it difficult for emergency vehicles to access and operate. Fire management in a desert environment may require specialized tactics because of how quickly a fire can spread in these dry conditions.

A notable case occurred at Cairo International Airport, where a fire broke out on a cargo plane in a desert area. Fire crews, equipped with specialized terrain trucks, were able to contain the fire in less than 15 minutes, thanks to prior preparation and knowledge of desert conditions (CAA, 2019). This event demonstrates the need for site-specific strategies, including familiarization with terrain characteristics.

## Water Bodies

Bodies of water, such as rivers and lakes, are also considered difficult locations, especially in the vicinity of an airport. While they can provide useful resources for firefighting, their presence can also complicate operations. Aircraft landing on or near bodies of water may encounter hazardous situations, such as the risk of sinking or difficulty in accessing victims.

At San Juan International Airport, Puerto Rico, an incident in 2020 involved a crash landing in a body of water. Firefighters, being prepared to operate in these conditions, were able to use rescue boats to quickly access the aircraft passengers and conduct a safe evacuation (FAA, 2020). The ability of crews to work in bodies of water underscores the importance of planning and training in different environments.

## TACTICS AND STRATEGIES FOR AIRCRAFT FIREFIGHTING

### Mangroves

Mangroves, which are found in coastal areas, present another type of challenge. This type of ecosystem is vital for environmental protection, but its dense vegetation and limited access can make rescue and firefighting operations difficult. Firefighters must be able to navigate the uneven terrain and deal with wildlife that may pose a risk.

A success story occurred at Havana International Airport, Cuba, where an aircraft caught fire in the vicinity of a mangrove swamp. Emergency crews, equipped with knowledge of the ecosystem and access routes, were able to contain the fire and evacuate passengers without loss of life (Cuba Civil Aviation Institute, 2021). This incident highlights the importance of local ecology training for effective response.

### Mountains

Mountains are another difficult terrain that can be encountered in the vicinity of airports. The rugged terrain, altitude and changing weather conditions can significantly complicate emergency response. In situations where an aircraft crashes in mountainous areas, access can be extremely limited.

One notable incident was the crash of a passenger plane in the Peruvian Andes, where access to the area was very complicated due to the characteristics of the terrain. Rescue teams, who had been trained to operate in mountains, managed to reach the crash site using climbing techniques and specialized vehicles, managing to rescue the survivors (Peruvian Air Force, 2018). This event highlights the need for specific preparation for operations in mountainous terrain.

# TACTICS AND STRATEGIES FOR AIRCRAFT FIREFIGHTING

## Importance for Aircraft Rescue Firefighters

The identification of these difficult locations and their evaluation is crucial for Aircraft Rescue Firefighters for several reasons:

1. **Strategic Planning**: Understanding the location of difficult locations allows fire crews to develop more effective response plans. This includes creating alternate routes and identifying access points that can be used if primary routes are not available.
2. **Training and Drills**: Regular training that includes emergency scenarios in difficult locations is essential. Firefighters must be familiar with the challenges presented by these locations to be able to act quickly and effectively during a crisis.
3. **Resource Optimization**: Knowing the constraints of difficult sites allows teams to allocate resources more effectively, ensuring that the right equipment is available in the right place at the right time.

## Regulations and Recommendations

**NFPA 409** and **ICAO** provide guidelines that can help airports plan and manage hardscapes. NFPA emphasizes the importance of accessibility and the need to maintain clear routes for access to all areas of the airport, while ICAO sets standards for airport design that minimize risks associated with difficult access areas (NFPA, 2020; ICAO Annex 14, 2019).

## Success Stories in Real Emergencies

A prime example of the importance of planning in difficult locations was at Orlando International Airport, where an aircraft fire during takeoff required rapid intervention. Despite the difficult location of the aircraft, which was near a wooded area, firefighters were able to gain rapid access thanks to a response plan that included alternate access routes and the use of firefighting vehicles designed for difficult terrain. This approach effectively brought the fire under control and safeguarded all passengers on board (FAA, 2018).

Another notable incident occurred at San Francisco International Airport in 2017. During an aircraft cabin smoke evacuation, access was complicated due to the lay of the terrain and nearby structures. However, firefighters used a combination of off-road vehicles and difficult terrain navigation skills to reach the aircraft and secure the evacuation of passengers. This event highlighted the importance of proper preparation and prior knowledge of problem areas (FAA, 2017).

### Strategies for the Management of Difficult Sites

To optimize response in difficult locations, the following strategies should be implemented:

1.  **Risk Assessment**: Conduct a risk assessment at the airport that identifies difficult sites and establishes a specific action plan for each one.
2.  **Infrastructure Design**: Plan airport infrastructure in a manner that minimizes difficult locations, including the construction of adequate roads and the removal of unnecessary obstacles.
3.  **Specialized Equipment**: Equip firefighting teams with vehicles and equipment that are capable of operating in difficult terrain, such as off-road fire trucks and portable firefighting equipment.
4.  **Ongoing Training**: Invest in regular training that includes drills in difficult locations, ensuring that firefighters are prepared to meet any challenge that arises during an emergency.

### 1.1.6 Water Intake Points for Equipment Replenishment

The ability of Aircraft Rescue Firefighters to respond effectively to aircraft fires is highly dependent on their access to water sources. Proper planning of water intake points is essential to ensure that firefighting teams can be quickly resupplied during an emergency. This section will explore the importance of these water intake points, their strategic location and success stories that highlight their relevance in emergency situations.

**Importance of Water Intake Points**

Water intake points are critical for several reasons:

1. **Quick Access to Resources**: In fire situations, time is a critical factor. The availability of nearby water intake points allows fire crews to resupply their firefighting trucks quickly and efficiently, which can be critical in controlling a fire before it spreads.
2. **Responsiveness**: The strategic location of water intake points within the airport ensures that emergency vehicles can access them without hindrance, even in emergency situations. NFPA states that emergency facilities should have access to sufficient water in a timely manner (NFPA, 2020).
3. **Planning for Different Scenarios**: Firefighters must be prepared for different types of fires that may require different extinguishing methods. The availability of water, along with other extinguishing agents, allows for a more versatile and effective response.

**Regulations and Recommendations**

**NFPA 409** and **ICAO** provide guidelines on the installation of water intake points at airports. According to NFPA, it is essential that these points be designed to withstand the load of emergency vehicles and be easily accessible. **ICAO** also stresses the importance of ensuring an adequate supply of water for fire suppression at all airport facilities (ICAO Annex 14, 2019).

### Types of Water Intake Points

Water intake points can be classified into several categories:

1.  **Water Hydrants**: These are essential for resupplying fire vehicles and should be strategically distributed throughout the airport. The NFPA recommends a location that allows quick access from multiple directions.
2.  **Natural Water Bodies**: Nearby rivers, lakes or ponds can serve as water sources in emergencies. However, their use may require special equipment for water collection and transport.
3.  **Storage Tanks**: Some airports have water storage tanks designed specifically for emergencies. These tanks should be located near the airside to ensure quick access.

### Success Stories in Real Emergencies

A prominent case that illustrates the importance of water intake points is the Asiana Airlines Flight 214 fire at San Francisco International Airport in 2013. During this incident, firefighters were able to quickly refuel their vehicles from a well-designed hydrant system, allowing them to contain the fire on the aircraft and prevent it from spreading to the terminal (FAA, 2014). Planning and proper infrastructure played a crucial role in the response to this incident.

Another example occurred at Denver Airport in 2019, when an airliner had an incident that generated smoke in the cabin. Firefighters, by utilizing a nearby water intake point, were able to quickly refuel and bring the fire under control within minutes. This success highlighted the importance of having strategically located and accessible water points for efficient response (Denver Fire Department, 2019).

## Strategies for Water Point Intake Planning

To maximize the effectiveness of water intake points, the following strategies should be implemented:

1.  **Site Assessment**: Conduct a terrain and airport layout analysis to identify optimal locations for water intake points, considering access and proximity to areas of highest risk.
2.  **Regular Maintenance**: Implement a maintenance program to ensure that hydrants and other water intake points are always operational and accessible. This includes periodic flushing and testing of water systems.
3.  **Personnel Training**: Ensure that all fire team members are familiar with the location and operation of water intake points and procedures for their use in emergencies.
4.  **Integration with Other Infrastructure**: Water intake points should be integrated into airport emergency plans, ensuring that there is clear communication between fire crews and other emergency services about their location and availability.

## 1.1.7 Number of Runways and Distance to the Farthest Parts of the Airport

Airport infrastructure is a critical factor in emergency response to aircraft fires. In this regard, the number of runways and the distance to the farthest parts of the airport are key elements to be considered by Aircraft Rescue Firefighters. This section explores the importance of these aspects in the planning and execution of firefighting operations, based on **National Fire Protection Association (NFPA), International Civil Aviation Organization (ICAO)** and **Federal Aviation Administration (FAA)** regulations.

# TACTICS AND STRATEGIES FOR AIRCRAFT FIREFIGHTING

## Number of Tracks and their Relevance

The number of runways at an airport directly affects the operation and emergency management. Airports with multiple runways can handle a higher volume of air traffic, which increases the likelihood of incidents and emergencies. Therefore, it is essential that fire crews are well prepared to respond to situations on any of these runways.

1. **Rapid Access**: The number of runways determines how quickly emergency vehicles can reach the scene of an incident. At a large airport with multiple runways, it is vital that access routes are clearly defined and easily navigated. The NFPA states that emergency crews must be able to access any runway in a minimum amount of time to contain any fire that may arise (NFPA, 2020).
2. **Drills and Training**: Firefighters must be trained to respond to incidents on different runways, which includes familiarization with the routes and equipment needed to operate on each runway. Regular training is crucial to ensure an effective response.

## Distance to the Farthest Parts of the Airport

The distance between runways and the farthest area of the airport is another critical factor in emergency response planning. As an airport expands, there may be areas that are significantly distant from firefighting facilities. This can affect response time and fire containment effectiveness.

1. **Distance Analysis**: NFPA recommends that firefighting facilities be strategically located to cover all areas of the airport. This includes a distance analysis to determine the response time to the most distant parts (NFPA 409, 2020).
2. **Route Establishment**: Planning efficient access routes is essential to ensure that emergency vehicles can reach the most remote areas in the shortest possible time. This may

include the creation of dedicated roads that are exclusive for emergency vehicle use.

## Success Stories in Real Emergencies

A notable case illustrating the importance of the number of runways and the distance to the far reaches of the airport occurred at O'Hare International Airport in Chicago, where a plane crashed on one of the runways during a failed landing. Due to the number of runways and efficient route planning, firefighters were able to quickly access the crash site from several directions, allowing them to effectively control the fire and perform the necessary evacuations (FAA, 2015).

Another example occurred at Los Angeles International Airport, where an incident involved a fire in the cockpit of an aircraft on one of the runways. Although the aircraft was in a location relatively far from fire facilities, pre-planning and knowledge of access routes allowed crews to quickly reach the scene of the fire and contain it within minutes, preventing additional damage and ensuring the safety of passengers and crew (LAFD, 2018).

## Strategies to Improve Emergency Response

To optimize fire response effectiveness, several strategies should be implemented in relation to the number of tracks and the distance to the farthest areas:

1. **Ongoing Assessment**: Conduct periodic assessments of airport infrastructure to identify areas that may present challenges in terms of distance and access.
2. **Emergency Drills**: Conduct regular drills that include response scenarios on different runways and areas of the airport. This will help firefighters become familiar with routes and improve coordination between response teams.
3. **Technology Development**: Implement technologies that facilitate navigation and access to the runways. This may

include digital signage systems and mobile applications that
provide real-time information on access routes and
emergency locations.

4. **Distance Management Training**: Train fire crews in
distance management and response times, ensuring they
understand how to optimize their movements to minimize
response time in critical situations.

## 1.1.8 Structures Involved in Accidents Occur in the 5 Nautical Mile Zone of Influence

The zone of influence of an airport, defined as a radius of 5 nautical
miles (approximately 9.26 kilometers), includes not only the nearby
airspace, but also a set of structures that could be involved in the
event of an accident. The characteristics of the structures located in
this zone can significantly influence the response of Aircraft Rescue
Firefighters. This discussion will address the different types of
structures within this area, how they impact emergency operations,
and factors that firefighters should consider when planning their
response.

### Types of Structures in the Zone of Influence

1. **Residential Buildings**: In many urban and suburban areas
near airports, there are residential developments that fall
within the zone of influence. These buildings pose a
significant risk in the event of an accident, both because of
the potential for direct damage and the need to evacuate
residents quickly. Firefighters must be aware of the
proximity of these areas to coordinate a response that
focuses not only on the stricken aircraft, but also on the
protection of the civilian population.
2. **Critical Infrastructure**: Roads, railways, bridges and other
critical infrastructure may also be present in this area. Quick
access to these structures is crucial not only for firefighters,
but also for other emergency services. A plane crash
occurring near a major highway could block access routes,

requiring advanced logistical planning to ensure that emergency crews can reach the site efficiently.

3.  **Commercial and Industrial Facilities**: Commercial and industrial areas are located within the catchment area of many international airports. These structures may contain hazardous materials or be designed in such a way as to present an additional risk in the event of an accident. For example, industrial facilities may house flammable chemicals, which could increase the severity of a fire or explosion associated with an aircraft accident.

4.  **Public and Educational Buildings**: Schools, hospitals and other public facilities may also be within the 5 nautical mile zone of influence. These buildings require special attention in emergency planning, as they often house large numbers of people, including those who may have difficulty evacuating quickly, such as children, the elderly, or people with disabilities.

## Importance for Aircraft Rescue Firefighters

The presence of these structures within the area of influence of an airport has a direct impact on the planning and execution of aeronautical firefighter operations:

1.  **Interagency Coordination**: Aircraft Rescue Firefighters do not operate in isolation, especially in accidents involving areas outside the airport perimeter. They must coordinate with local fire departments, emergency medical services, police and civil authorities to ensure that all areas at risk, including adjacent structures, are adequately addressed.

2.  **Evacuation Planning**: In the event of accidents involving residential areas or public facilities, rapid and safe evacuation is a priority. Aircraft Rescue Firefighters should be familiar with evacuation procedures for these buildings, as well as escape routes and safe assembly points.

3.  **Specific Training**: Given the variety of structures that may be found in the zone of influence, firefighters should

receive specific training on how to respond to emergencies in different types of buildings. This includes knowledge of the fire resistance of structures, the presence of hazardous materials, and rescue procedures in facilities with high occupant density.

## Success Stories in Real Emergencies

A prime example of the importance of planning for Aircraft Rescue Firefighters in the catchment area is the 2001 crash of American Airlines Flight 587, which crashed in a residential area of Belle Harbor, New York, shortly after takeoff from John F. Kennedy International Airport. New York City firefighters, along with airport crews, worked in coordination to extinguish the fire that consumed several homes, evacuate residents, and mitigate the risk of additional explosions due to burning debris from the aircraft (NTSB, 2004). This incident underscored the importance of having an integrated strategy for responding to both the aircraft crash and collateral damage to residential structures.

Another significant example is the crash of Air Florida Flight 90 in 1982, which crashed into the Potomac River near Washington National Airport. Although the aircraft impacted the water, its proximity to bridges and major highways complicated the emergency response. Firefighters, along with other rescue services, had to use boats and helicopters to quickly reach the crash site, demonstrating the need for flexibility and adaptation in responding to incidents in areas with critical infrastructure (FAA, 1983).

## Strategies to Optimize Response

To improve accident response in the 5 nautical mile (9.2 kilometer) zone of influence, it is essential to implement the following strategies:

## TACTICS AND STRATEGIES FOR AIRCRAFT FIREFIGHTING

1. **Hazard Mapping**: Aeronautical fire crews should have detailed maps of the zone of influence that include all critical structures. This mapping should be updated regularly to reflect any new developments in the region.
2. **Multidisciplinary Drills**: Emergency drills involving accidents in areas outside the airport should involve multiple institutions, such as local fire departments, police and medical services. These drills will help all actors to better understand their roles and improve coordination in emergency situations.
3. **Response Technology**: New technologies, such as drones and real-time mapping systems, can significantly improve firefighters' ability to quickly assess an accident scene and determine which structures are most at risk. These technological resources can also facilitate damage assessment and identification of blocked access routes.

### 1.1.9 Behavior in Various Weather Conditions

Weather conditions play a crucial role in fire behavior and the operability of emergency crews. Some of the main weather conditions and their impact on aeronautical firefighter operations are described below.

1. **High Temperature Conditions**: High temperatures not only affect the physical performance of personnel but can also accelerate the spread of fire. In extreme conditions, equipment can overheat, and firefighters must be prepared to deal with fatigue. In these scenarios, the use of cooling systems for equipment and frequent rotation of personnel are key strategies to maintain operability.
2. **Low Temperature and Snow Conditions**: Ice and snow can significantly complicate firefighter operations. Slippery slopes and ice-covered roads make access difficult, and equipment can freeze, affecting its functionality. Firefighters in cold climates must be equipped with

specialized clothing and equipment to maintain operability in these conditions.

An example of a cold weather emergency occurred in 1982, when Air Florida Flight 90 crashed into the Potomac River during a snowstorm. Cold temperatures and ice complicated rescue efforts, but preparation and the use of specialized equipment, such as helicopters and immersion suits, saved several survivors (FAA, 1983).

3. **High Winds and Thunderstorms**: Wind can spread fire quickly, requiring firefighters to adjust their strategies based on wind direction. Thunderstorms can also pose an additional hazard to emergency operations, increasing the risk of secondary fires or communications disruptions.

### Strategies for Addressing Terrain and Climate Challenges

To mitigate the challenges presented by the different types of terrain and climatic conditions, several strategies must be implemented:

1. **Specific Training**: Firefighters should receive specific training to operate in the types of terrain prevalent at the airports where they work. This includes training in mountain rescue, use of off-road vehicles, and operations in water or flooded areas.
2. **Specialized Equipment**: Having the right equipment is crucial for operating in different types of terrain and weather conditions. Airports in cold climates must be equipped with ice-resistant rescue vehicles and suits, while airports in warm areas must have cooling systems for personnel and equipment.
3. **Ongoing Risk Assessments**: It is important to conduct regular assessments of terrain and weather conditions, using monitoring and forecasting technology to anticipate difficulties that could arise in a rescue.

## 1.1.10 Critical Areas Within the Airport for the Presence of Hazardous Materials

The presence of hazardous materials (HAZMAT) within an airport represents one of the most significant challenges for Aircraft Rescue Firefighters. Critical areas where these materials are stored or handled require rigorous planning and specialized training to ensure an effective emergency response. This analysis explores the areas within an airport that

are considered critical due to the presence of hazardous materials, how these risks are managed, and how firefighters should prepare to act in these situations.

### Types of Hazardous Materials at an Airport

1.  **Aviation Fuels**: Fuels used in aviation, such as Jet-A and aviation gasoline (AVGAS), are highly flammable and are stored in large quantities in tanks within the airport. These tanks pose a high risk in the event of a fire or spill, so firefighters must be trained in specialized fuel fire containment techniques.
2.  **Chemical Materials**: Airports often store chemicals for aircraft maintenance and other operations. These include solvents, cleaning products and chemicals used in aircraft decontamination and deicing. These materials can be toxic and volatile, increasing the risk of explosion or release of hazardous gases.
3.  **Radioactive Substances**: At some airports, especially those handling cargo flights, small quantities of radioactive materials may be transported. Although these materials are

securely packaged, any damage to the containers in an accident can present serious risks to the health and safety of emergency personnel.

4. **Explosives**: On military or cargo flights, some airports may handle explosives or ammunition. Although these materials are usually highly regulated, their presence greatly increases the level of danger in the event of an accident or fire.

Scan the QR code and you will see a video of the Aircraft Rescue Firefighters of Memphis International Airport (USA) called "ARFF Cargo Aircraft Firefighting".

### Critical Areas Inside the Airport

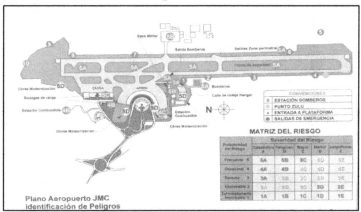

1. **Fuel Tanks**: Fuel tanks are some of the most critical areas within an airport. These tanks are usually located in peripheral areas of the airport to minimize the risk in case of fire, but their proximity to runways and terminals means that any incident in these areas could have catastrophic consequences. **NFPA 407** establishes strict regulations on

the storage and handling of fuels at airports, recommending the installation of automatic extinguishing systems and containment measures to prevent spills (NFPA, 2020).

2. **Loading and Unloading Areas**: Designated areas for loading and unloading of dangerous goods represent another critical point. Firefighters must be prepared to respond to emergencies involving hazardous materials, whether during the handling, storage, or transportation of these materials. **ICAO** stresses the importance of specific training in the management of incidents involving dangerous goods and establishes strict regulations to minimize risks (ICAO Annex 18, 2019).

3. **Maintenance Hangar**: Maintenance hangars house not only aircraft, but also a wide variety of hazardous materials used for aircraft maintenance and repair. From fuels to chemicals, firefighters must be aware of the specific hazards present in each hangar. **NFPA 409** provides clear guidelines

on the fire protection systems that should be installed in these spaces, including foam fire suppression systems and the installation of gas detectors (NFPA, 2020).

# TACTICS AND STRATEGIES FOR AIRCRAFT FIREFIGHTING

## How Aircraft Rescue Firefighters Handle These Risks

1. **Specialized Training**: Handling hazardous materials requires specialized training. Aircraft Rescue Firefighters must be trained not only in traditional firefighting techniques, but also in hazardous materials containment and neutralization procedures. This includes the use of special suits for protection against toxic materials and training in ventilation and decontamination systems.
2. **Detection and Suppression Systems**: Modern airports have advanced fire detection and hazardous gas release systems. These systems allow for rapid and automatic response in the event of a hazardous materials emergency. Firefighters must be familiar with the operation of these systems and know how to integrate them into their emergency operations.
3. **Coordination with Other Teams**: In the event of an emergency involving hazardous materials, Aircraft Rescue Firefighters are not likely to work alone. Coordination with other teams, such as HAZMAT specialists and health and safety authorities, is essential to mitigate risks. Joint drills are a key tool to ensure that all teams are prepared to work together effectively.

## Success Stories in Real Emergencies

An outstanding case highlighting the importance of emergency preparedness for hazardous material emergencies occurred at Hong Kong International Airport in 2002, when a fire started in a fuel storage facility. Despite the extreme risk due to the amount of fuel stored, firefighters were able to contain the fire due to their advanced training in fuel management and the use of automatic foam fire suppression systems. This incident underscored the importance of having well-established emergency plans for critical areas of the airport (CAA, 2003).

Another notable case occurred at Los Angeles International Airport in 2010, when a cargo plane carrying hazardous chemicals crashed on the runway. Firefighters, trained to handle hazardous materials, acted quickly to contain the chemical spills and prevent a major catastrophe. The use of protective suits and coordination with HAZMAT teams were essential to the success of the operation (FAA, 2011).

### Strategies for Optimizing Critical Area Security

To improve safety and responsiveness to hazardous materials incidents, several key strategies must be implemented:

1.  **Continuous Risk Assessments**: Airports should conduct regular risk assessments in all critical areas, with special attention to fuel depots, cargo areas and maintenance hangars. These assessments identify vulnerabilities and improve contingency plans.

2.  **Regular Drills**: Emergency drills involving hazardous materials should be conducted on a regular basis. These drills help firefighters become familiar with specific HAZMAT handling procedures and ensure that they are prepared to act in any situation.

3.  **Investment in Security Infrastructure**: The installation of advanced detection and suppression systems is essential to minimize the risks associated with hazardous materials. Airports must invest in technology that enables early detection of fires and spills, as well as systems that can

effectively contain these hazards before they become a major threat.

## 1.1.11 Quantities of Fuel Stored, Extinguishing Systems in Airport Infrastructure as well as in Storage Tanks

Fuel storage at an airport represents one of the most critical elements of airport security. The large volumes of fuel needed to supply flight operations make these areas high-risk zones that must be managed with extreme care. The planning and design of fire suppression systems in fuel storage infrastructures are essential to prevent catastrophes and ensure the protection of emergency equipment.

This section discusses the quantities of fuel stored at airports, the most appropriate extinguishing systems for storage tanks and how these aspects serve Aircraft Rescue Firefighters during emergency operations. In addition, success stories from real emergencies will be presented, highlighting the importance of having a well-designed infrastructure and adequate response procedures.

### Quantities of Fuel Stored in Airports

International airports handle enormous amounts of fuel, which vary depending on the size of the airport and the volume of air traffic. For example, large airports, such as Los Angeles International Airport (LAX), can store more than 150 million liters of fuel in subway and above-ground tanks. This fuel is stored in special tanks, generally located in areas away from passenger terminals, to reduce the risk in case of incidents.

**NFPA 30** regulates aspects related to the safe storage of flammable liquids, establishing safety requirements for the construction, layout and fire protection of storage tanks. These tanks are usually double-walled and equipped with leak detection systems to minimize risks.

## TACTICS AND STRATEGIES FOR AIRCRAFT FIREFIGHTING

The presence of large volumes of fuel requires continuous preparation by aviation firefighters, who must be familiar with storage systems and know how to respond to potential spills or fires. The high volatility of aviation fuel, such as Jet-A, means that even a small fire could escalate rapidly if not controlled quickly.

### Extinguishing Systems in Airport Infrastructures

The design and implementation of fire suppression systems are critical to protect fuel storage tanks at airports. Among the most common systems are:

1. **Foam Extinguishing Systems**: Foam systems are the most effective systems for fighting flammable liquid fires, such as jet fuel. These systems are usually high expansion and are designed to quickly cover large areas with a layer of foam that suffocates the fire by eliminating the oxygen needed for combustion. **NFPA 11** regulates the use of low-, medium-, and high-expansion foam in industrial and airport facilities, ensuring that the systems can deploy quickly enough to smother a fire before it spreads (NFPA, 2020).
2. **Automatic Sprinkler Systems**: Although automatic sprinkler systems are not as common in fuel tanks as foam systems, they can be used in adjacent areas, such as service buildings or smaller tanks. These systems automatically activate when they detect excessive heat, spraying water or chemicals to contain the fire.
3. **Fire Detection Systems**: Early detection is key to preventing a fire from spreading in fuel storage areas. Modern systems have temperature and smoke detectors as well as gas sensors that can identify dangerous leaks. Once a problem is detected, the systems can automatically activate alarms and extinguishing systems, notifying emergency crews.
4. **Containment Barriers**: In addition to fire suppression systems, fuel tanks are often equipped with physical barriers

that prevent the spread of fuel in the event of a spill. These barriers, known as containment dikes, are essential to reduce the risk of contamination and limit the spread of the fire.

## How These Systems Serve Aircraft Rescue Firefighters

Well-planned extinguishing systems and infrastructure provide a critical advantage to Aircraft Rescue Firefighters. By having automatic response systems in place, intervention time is significantly reduced and the risks of fire spreading to other areas of the airport are minimized.

1. **Reduced Response Time**: Automatic detection and extinguishing systems can start fighting a fire in seconds, even before firefighters arrive on the scene. This gives teams time to organize their response, prioritizing the protection of surrounding areas and ensuring that no casualties are endangered.
2. **Protection of Emergency Personnel**: Foam systems allow firefighters to work more safely, as foam suppresses heat and toxic gases, allowing for a more controlled intervention. In addition, fire containment prevents the fuel from continuing to burn and facilitates complete extinguishment.
3. **Spill and Expansion Control**: In the event of a fuel spill, containment systems, together with extinguishing systems, are essential to limit the affected area and prevent fuel from reaching other critical infrastructure, such as runways or terminal buildings.

## Success Stories in Real Emergencies

An emblematic case illustrating the importance of extinguishing systems in fuel storage areas occurred at London Heathrow International Airport in 2008, when a fuel tank exploded due to a technical failure. Thanks to automatic detection systems and high expansion foam systems installed in the tanks, the fire was quickly contained before it could affect nearby areas. The rapid intervention allowed firefighters to extinguish the fire without casualties or major damage to adjacent infrastructure (CAA, 2009).

Another relevant case was the incident at Denver International Airport in 2015, when a fire in a subway fuel tank was brought under control in less than 10 minutes thanks to the automatic activation of a foam system. This system not only prevented the fire from spreading, but also minimized the risk to fire crews arriving on the scene. The advanced safety infrastructure in Denver was key to the success of this operation (FAA, 2016).

Strategies to Improve Safety in Storage Tanks

To ensure effective incident response in fuel storage areas, the following strategies should be followed:

1.  **Maintenance and Updating of Systems**: Detection and extinguishing systems should be inspected and maintained regularly to ensure that they are in perfect working order. This includes testing of foam systems and calibration of gas and temperature sensors.
2.  **Regular Drills**: Emergency drills involving fires in fuel storage areas should be conducted on a **regular** basis, allowing firefighters to familiarize themselves with specific procedures and coordinate with other emergency teams.
3.  **Specialized Training**: Aircraft Rescue Firefighters must receive specialized training in the management of flammable material fires, as well as in the use of personal protective equipment and foam extinguishing systems.

### 1.1.12 Water and Foam Reserves

In airport emergency planning, water and foam reserves are fundamental elements to ensure an effective and rapid response to fires, especially in situations involving aircraft. Airports, due to the nature of aircraft operations and the presence of large quantities of fuels, need to have well-designed systems that provide an adequate supply of these resources. International regulations such as **NFPA 403** and the recommendations of the **International Civil Aviation Organization (ICAO)** require airports to have sufficient reserves to deal with emergencies without relying on external resources in the first critical minutes of a fire.

This section explores the importance of water and foam reserves at airports, how these reserves serve Aircraft Rescue Firefighters in their emergency response and presents success stories in which these resources played a crucial role in fire containment.

**Importance of Water and Foam Reservoirs**

1.  **Continuous Supply of Critical Resources**: During an aircraft fire, time is a critical factor. Aircraft Rescue Firefighters must have immediate access to sufficient quantities of water and foam to extinguish the fire as quickly as possible. **NFPA 403** states that airports must have the capability to provide an initial flush of water and foam sufficient to contain the fire for at least 15 minutes without interruption (NFPA, 2020).
2.  **Compatibility with Extinguishing Systems**: Airport fire suppression systems, especially foam systems are designed to interact with water supplies efficiently. Firefighters should be familiar with systems that use mixtures of water and foam, as well as the proper proportions of each resource depending on the type of fire, to maximize firefighting effectiveness.
3.  **Strategic Storage**: Water and foam reserves should be strategically stored around the airport for easy access in the event of an emergency. Storage points should be located near the runways and areas of greatest risk, such as fuel depots and hangars, ensuring that transport time to the incident site is kept to a minimum.

## TACTICS AND STRATEGIES FOR AIRCRAFT FIREFIGHTING

### Water Reserves

Water is the most basic and essential resource in firefighting. Airports must have water supply systems designed to provide sufficient quantities of this resource at all times, including:

1. **High Pressure Hydrants**: Airports should have a network of high-pressure hydrants strategically distributed throughout the critical infrastructure. These hydrants allow fire trucks to refill their tanks quickly during an emergency. According to **ICAO**, the minimum pressure in the hydrants must be sufficient to allow rapid recharge without interrupting ongoing firefighting operations (ICAO Annex 14, 2019).

2. **Water Reservoir Tanks**: Many airports supplement their hydrant system with water storage tanks dedicated exclusively to emergencies. These tanks should have the capacity to supply at least the volume needed to manage the most severe emergencies, such as wide-body aircraft fires, which require a large amount of water in a short period of time.

### Foam Reserves

Foam is an essential extinguishing agent for flammable liquid fires, such as aircraft fuel fires. Its ability to smother flames and block fuel evaporation makes it an indispensable resource for Aircraft Rescue Firefighters. Foam stocks include:

1. **Foam Proportioning Systems**: These systems mix water with the foaming agent in the proper proportions to generate low to medium expansion foam, which is effective in suppressing hydrocarbon fires. **NFPA 11** regulates the use and application of foam systems, ensuring that airports have adequate facilities to provide this extinguishing agent in copious quantities (NFPA, 2020).

2.  **Foam Storage Tanks**: Airports should maintain specific foam storage tanks that can be used quickly in case of emergency. These tanks are connected to emergency vehicles or fixed extinguishing systems, allowing for immediate response when faced with large fires.

How These Reserves Serve Aircraft Rescue Firefighters

1.  **Immediate Response and Continuity of Combat**: The availability of copious quantities of water and foam allows Aircraft Rescue Firefighters to initiate immediate and sustained firefighting. The speed with which they can deploy these resources is crucial to prevent a minor fire on an aircraft or at an airport facility from becoming a major disaster.
2.  **Complex Fire Management**: Aircraft fires often involve hazardous materials, such as highly flammable fuels. The use of foam in these situations is essential, as it not only extinguishes the flames, but also seals the fuel, preventing flammable vapors from being released again. This reduces the risk of reignition, which facilitates the work of firefighters.
3.  **Minimizing Damage to Critical Infrastructure**: Adequate water and foam reserves not only help extinguish aircraft fires, but are also essential to protect critical airport infrastructure such as hangars, terminals and fuel depots. Keeping these areas safe is crucial to prevent long-term damage and ensure the continuity of airport operations.

**Success Stories in Real Emergencies**

A prime example of the critical role played by water and foam reserves occurred during the fire on British Airways Flight 38 at Heathrow International Airport in 2008. After the aircraft suffered a mechanical failure and made an emergency landing, the engine began to catch fire. Thanks to strategically placed foam reserves and the rapid intervention of firefighters, the fire was quickly contained without spreading to the aircraft fuselage or adjacent facilities (CAA, 2009). This case highlights the importance of having sufficient foam reserves near runways and critical points of the airport.

Another relevant case is the Asiana Airlines Flight 214 incident at San Francisco International Airport in 2013. After the aircraft crashed during landing, a fire broke out in the fuselage. Aircraft Rescue Firefighters used both water and foam in large quantities to control the fire. The immediate availability of these resources contained the fire and saved numerous lives (FAA, 2014).

### Strategies to Improve the Use of Water and Foam Reservoirs

To optimize the use of water and foam reserves at airports, several strategies need to be implemented:

1. **Maintenance of Storage Systems**: Water and foam storage systems should be inspected and maintained regularly to ensure that they are fully functional in the event of an emergency. This includes checking hydrant pressures, cleaning tanks, and checking foam mixing systems.
2. **Emergency Drills**: Regular emergency drills allow Aircraft Rescue Firefighters to practice the use of water and foam systems in realistic situations. These exercises are essential to identify areas for improvement and ensure that personnel are fully trained in the use of these resources.
3. **Updating Reserves**: As airports grow and handle larger and more complex aircraft, it is essential that water and foam reserves are updated to meet operational needs. Airports should regularly assess whether their current reserves are sufficient to handle large fires and make adjustments as needed.

# TACTICS AND STRATEGIES FOR AIRCRAFT FIREFIGHTING

## 1.1.13 Familiarization with Aircraft and their Importance in Performing a Preliminary Analysis

Familiarization with aircraft is a crucial element for aeronautical firefighting teams, as it allows them to be adequately prepared for emergencies that may occur at an airport. A detailed knowledge of the specific characteristics of each aircraft, its internal systems and general structure is key to anticipate risk scenarios and respond effectively and efficiently. International standards, including NFPA 403 (2022), International Civil Aviation Organization (ICAO) annexes, and Federal Aviation Administration (FAA) regulations, underscore the importance of this knowledge for safe emergency operations (NFPA, 2022; ICAO, 2019).

### The Importance of Aircraft Familiarization

One of the most critical aspects of familiarization is the knowledge of the different aircraft models and their specificities, which allows Aircraft Rescue Firefighters to act quickly and efficiently in emergency situations. Key aspects to be familiarized include evacuation routes, fuel systems, battery tank locations and internal extinguishing systems. Periodic training with real or simulated aircraft, as required by NFPA 403 and ICAO and FAA regulations, reinforces the skills needed to quickly identify these components, which is vital in making quick and accurate decisions in an emergency situation (NFPA, 2022; ICAO, 2019).

Prior analysis of the aircraft allows firefighters to identify critical areas, such as the flight deck, passenger compartments and cargo holds, which are priority areas in a rescue. Reaction times in emergency situations are extremely limited; therefore, familiarization with the internal layout of aircraft, as well as door opening systems and emergency mechanisms, allows rescue teams to perform the necessary operations quickly and safely (FAA, 2020).

# TACTICS AND STRATEGIES FOR AIRCRAFT FIREFIGHTING

## Case Studies and Real Examples

An example of the importance of aircraft familiarization is the Asiana Airlines Flight 214 incident at San Francisco International Airport in 2013. During this event, the Boeing 777 aircraft crashed on final approach, resulting in a fire on board. The firefighters' response was quick and effective, due to specific training on aircraft of this type. The knowledge gained from previous training on the aircraft structure, including the location of exits and fuel systems, enabled responders to control the fire and evacuate passengers more quickly, minimizing loss of life (NTSB, 2014).

In another case, in the 2015 crash of British Airways Flight 2276 in Las Vegas, a Boeing 777 suffered a catastrophic engine failure during takeoff, resulting in a fire on the left wing. Firefighters responding to the incident were already familiar with the specifics of the aircraft model and were able to apply the correct firefighting techniques to critical areas, resulting in rapid fire control and protection of lives on board (FAA, 2020).

## Training and Education

NFPA 403 (2022) requires that Aircraft Rescue Firefighters receive periodic training that includes familiarization with the different types of aircraft using the airport. In addition, ICAO annexes highlight the importance of conducting aircraft drills, either virtually or physically, to reinforce the operational and tactical knowledge of emergency personnel (ICAO, 2019). This training not only covers aircraft structure, but also internal safety systems, such as onboard fire suppression systems, electrical controls, and fuel systems.

The use of simulators and training with decommissioned aircraft has also proven to be an effective tool for aeronautical fire crews to gain invaluable hands-on experience. This ensures that personnel can quickly adapt to technological changes in aircraft designs, an especially important factor given the constant advancement of the aviation industry (NFPA, 2022).

## TACTICS AND STRATEGIES FOR AIRCRAFT FIREFIGHTING

## Conclusions

Knowledge of the load carrying capacity of airport bridges and ramps is essential to the effectiveness of aeronautical fire crews. Regulations established by NFPA and ICAO not only dictate the construction and maintenance of these infrastructures, but also provide a framework for emergency preparedness. Lessons learned from actual incidents demonstrate that proper planning and a thorough understanding of load carrying capacity can make a difference in the effectiveness of emergency response.

Knowledge and understanding of rapid and critical access areas are essential to the effectiveness of Aircraft Rescue Firefighters. NFPA and ICAO standards provide a vital framework that guides the design and operation of airport infrastructures. Success stories in real emergencies highlight the importance of these areas, demonstrating how proper planning can save lives and mitigate damage in critical situations.

It is imperative that emergency responders continue their education and training in these areas, ensuring that they are prepared to act quickly and effectively when emergency situations arise.

Knowledge of the types of structures and their fire resistance is essential for the safety and effectiveness of Aircraft Rescue Firefighters. The regulations established by NFPA and ICAO provide a vital framework that guides the design and operation of airport infrastructures. Success stories in real emergencies highlight how proper fire resistance can save lives and mitigate damage in critical situations.

Response teams must continue their training in this area, ensuring that they are prepared to act effectively when faced with emergency situations in the various airport structures.

## TACTICS AND STRATEGIES FOR AIRCRAFT FIREFIGHTING

Perimeter roadways are a crucial element of airport infrastructure, providing the necessary access for rapid and effective response by Aircraft Rescue Firefighters. NFPA and ICAO standards establish guidelines to ensure that these roadways are suitable for emergency use. Success stories in real-world situations highlight how effective planning and design can save lives and reduce injuries. Implementing optimization strategies is essential to ensure that perimeter roadways remain a reliable resource for emergency crews.

Familiarity with the difficult terrain surrounding an airport is essential to the effectiveness of Aircraft Rescue Firefighters. The unique conditions of each environment require proper planning and preparation, as well as ongoing training of emergency responders. **NFPA** and **ICAO** regulations provide guidelines that are critical to managing these challenges, ensuring that teams are equipped and prepared to respond effectively to any situation.

Success stories in real emergencies demonstrate that preparedness and knowledge of the environment can make a significant difference in the safety and effectiveness of emergency response at airports. It is imperative that Aircraft Rescue Firefighters continue to train in these areas to ensure their ability to respond to any eventuality.

The planning and availability of water intake points are essential to the effectiveness of Aircraft Rescue Firefighters in emergency situations. NFPA and ICAO regulations provide a fundamental framework to ensure that these infrastructures are well designed and located. Success stories in real emergencies highlight the importance of preparedness and rapid access to resources, which can make all the difference in controlling fires and saving lives.

The number of runways and the distance to the farthest parts of the airport are crucial factors in the planning and execution of aeronautical firefighter operations. NFPA and ICAO regulations provide a vital framework to ensure that emergency crews are well prepared to deal with any situation at the airport. Success stories from actual emergencies highlight the importance of proper planning and ongoing training to ensure effective incident response.

The proximity of critical structures within five nautical miles of an airport is a significant challenge for Aircraft Rescue Firefighters. Proper planning, ongoing training and interagency coordination are essential to ensure an effective response to accidents in these areas. Success stories in real emergencies highlight the importance of being prepared to handle not only the aircraft accident itself, but also the risks associated with nearby structures.

The nature of the terrain and weather conditions are determining factors in the planning and execution of aeronautical firefighter operations. Proper preparation, including specific training and the necessary equipment, is essential to successfully meet the challenges presented by these environments. Success stories in real emergencies underscore the importance of strategic planning that takes terrain and weather into account.

Critical areas within an airport that house hazardous materials present a significant challenge for Aircraft Rescue Firefighters. Adequate preparation, including specialized training, advanced safety systems and coordination with other emergency teams, is essential to ensure an effective response to incidents involving hazardous materials. Success stories in real emergencies demonstrate that careful planning and rapid response can prevent major disasters and protect both people and infrastructure.

The amount of fuel stored at airports and the extinguishing systems in storage tanks are crucial factors in airport safety. Automatic detection and extinguishing systems provide a fast and effective response that can make the difference between a controlled fire and a catastrophe. Aircraft Rescue Firefighters must be familiar with these infrastructures and receive the necessary training to handle critical situations safely and efficiently.

## TACTICS AND STRATEGIES FOR AIRCRAFT FIREFIGHTING

Water and foam reserves are vital components in airport firefighting. Proper planning of these resources, along with specialized infrastructure and equipment, enables Aircraft Rescue Firefighters to respond quickly and effectively to emergencies. Success stories in real fires demonstrate that having an adequate supply of water and foam can be the difference between a controlled emergency and a major disaster. Ongoing training and regular maintenance are key to ensuring that these resources are always available when needed.

In conclusion, aircraft familiarization is an essential component of preparing Aircraft Rescue Firefighters to respond effectively to airport emergencies. Detailed aircraft knowledge, combined with periodic training and realistic simulations, not only improves personnel response capabilities, but also significantly increases passenger and crew safety. The above success stories demonstrate that proper training can make all the difference in the outcome of an emergency. As such, compliance with international regulations established by NFPA, ICAO and FAA is indispensable to ensure safe airport operations (NFPA, 2022; ICAO, 2019; FAA, 2020).

## TACTICS AND STRATEGIES FOR AIRCRAFT FIREFIGHTING

### References

NFPA 403: Standard for Aircraft Rescue and Fire-Fighting Services at Airports.

FAA Advisory Circular 150/5210-6D.

National Fire Protection Association (NFPA). (2020). NFPA 409: Standard on Aircraft Hangars. NFPA.

International Civil Aviation Organization (ICAO), (2019). Annex 14: Aerodromes, Volume I - Aerodrome Design and Operations. ICAO.

Federal Aviation Administration (FAA). (2002). Aircraft Fire and Rescue. FAA.

National Fire Protection Association (NFPA). (2020). *NFPA 5000: Building Construction and Safety Code*. NFPA.

ANAC. (2017). Plane crash in the Amazon jungle. National Civil Aviation Agency.

CAA. (2019). Report on the fire at Cairo International Airport. Civil Aviation Authority.

FAA (2020). Body of water rescues: procedures and success stories. Federal Aviation Administration.

Cuba Civil Aviation Institute (2021). Plane crash in mangroves near Havana International Airport. Cuban Civil Aviation Institute.

Peruvian Air Force (2018). Mountain rescue: case of the plane crash in the Andes. Peruvian Air Force.

Denver Fire Department (2019). Incident Report: Aircraft Emergency Response. Denver Fire Department.

Federal Aviation Administration (FAA). (2015). Incident Report: Aircraft Accident at O'Hare International Airport. FAA.

Los Angeles Fire Department (LAFD). (2018). Emergency Response Report: Aircraft Fire at Los Angeles International Airport. LAFD.

National Transportation Safety Board (NTSB) (2004). Aircraft Accident Report: American Airlines Flight 587. NTSB.
Federal Aviation Administration (FAA). (1983). Report on the Air Florida Flight 90 Accident. FAA.

National Fire Protection Association (NFPA). (2020). NFPA 407: Standard for Aircraft Fuel Servicing. NFPA.

International Civil Aviation Organization (ICAO), (2019). Annex 18: The Safe Transport of Dangerous Goods by Air. ICAO.

Civil Aviation Authority (CAA). (2003). Incident Report: Fuel Fire at Hong Kong International Airport. CAA.

Federal Aviation Administration (FAA). (2011). Report on the LAX Cargo Chemical Incident. FAA.

National Fire Protection Association (NFPA). (2020). NFPA 11: Standard for Low-, Medium-, and High-Expansion Foam Systems. NFPA.

Civil Aviation Authority (CAA). (2009). Incident Report: Fuel Tank Fire at Heathrow Airport. CAA.

Federal Aviation Administration (FAA). (2016). Denver Airport Fuel Fire Incident Report. FAA.

National Fire Protection Association (NFPA). (2020). NFPA 11: Standard for Low-, Medium-, and High-Expansion Foam Systems. NFPA.

Civil Aviation Authority (CAA). (2009). Incident Report: British Airways Flight 38 at Heathrow Airport. CAA.

Federal Aviation Administration (FAA). (2014). Asiana Airlines Flight 214 Accident Report. FAA.

# CHAPTER 2

# RESPONSE PLANNING

## TACTICS AND STRATEGIES FOR AIRCRAFT FIREFIGHTING

## INTRODUCTION

Response planning is one of the key elements in ensuring rapid and effective response to aeronautical emergencies. Advance preparation not only allows aeronautical fire personnel to act with greater safety and confidence, but also optimizes reaction times, which is crucial in situations where every second counts. The success of any response operation is built on detailed and well-informed planning based on airport analysis, as we discussed in Chapter 1.

The airport analysis, addressed previously, provides a comprehensive view of the physical and operational characteristics of the airport environment. This analysis provides a thorough understanding of critical areas, aircraft types, structures, access roads, environmental hazards and available resources. Without this initial assessment phase, response planning would lack a solid foundation, which could compromise both the safety of emergency personnel and the effectiveness of operations. Thus, all of the lessons learned from the previous analysis must be systematically and strategically incorporated into response plans and protocols.

Response planning, as established in NFPA 424 (2022) and Annexes 14 and 19 of the International Civil Aviation Organization (ICAO), should include the drafting of specific procedures for different types of incidents, such as aircraft fires, aircraft accidents, fuel spills and hazardous materials emergencies (ICAO, 2022; NFPA, 2022). These procedures should detail the actions that each team member should follow, with emphasis on coordination between the different actors involved, from first responders to external institutions.

In addition, it is essential to define clear protocols for each type of incident, specifying the role of each team, rapid access routes, critical intervention points and evacuation zones. Interagency collaboration also plays an essential role, so planning should incorporate mutual aid agreements between different entities, such as municipal fire departments, airport health and safety personnel, and regional response teams (NFPA 424, 2022).

# TACTICS AND STRATEGIES FOR AIRCRAFT FIREFIGHTING

In logistical terms, response planning should include detailed inventories of available and potentially available resources, including firefighting equipment, specialized vehicles, communication systems, and fire control and rescue materials. The identification and constant updating of these inventories are vital to ensure that the necessary resources are ready and available in the event of an emergency (FAA, 2021).

In conclusion, response planning is a continuous process that depends on a detailed analysis of the airport and the aircraft landing at it. From this basic knowledge, it is possible to start planning the critical areas and the quantities of extinguishing agents      that will be required to solve the emergency.

Only through a clear understanding of        the operating environment, specific hazards and available resources can Aircraft Rescue

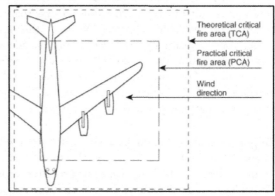

Firefighters develop action plans that are effective and efficient. This chapter will seek to develop key principles and strategies for the development of emergency plans that meet international standards and ensure a coordinated and successful response to any type of aeronautical incident.

## 2.1 Incident Command System Overview

The Incident Command System (ICS) is a standardized organizational structure designed to ensure efficient and coordinated emergency management, providing a comprehensive response to any type of incident, including aeronautical emergencies. The ICS enables Aircraft Rescue Firefighters, together with other emergency services, to act quickly, in a structured and effective manner, even in high-pressure situations such as aircraft fires, runway collisions, fuel spills or hazardous materials incidents.

The ICS was initially developed in the United States in response to the wildfires that affected the state of California in the 1970s. Since then, it has evolved to become the worldwide reference system for incident management, being adopted and standardized by international organizations such as the International Civil Aviation Organization (ICAO), the Federal Aviation Administration (FAA) and the National Fire Protection Association (NFPA) (NFPA 1561, 2022; FAA, 2020). In the airport context, the ICS is essential to effectively coordinate the different institutions involved in an aeronautical emergency, ensuring the integration of resources and rapid decision making.

## Incident Command System Structure and Principles

The ICS is based on a modular and scalable organizational structure, allowing it to adjust to the size and complexity of the incident. This flexibility is critical in the airport environment, where emergencies can range from minor incidents to major disasters. One of the key principles of the ICS is the clear assignment of roles and responsibilities, which minimizes confusion and ensures that everyone involved in the response operation understands their specific tasks (NFPA 1561, 2022).

In an aeronautical emergency, the Incident Commander has overall responsibility for incident management. This role includes coordination of the response teams, key decision making and implementation of the action plan. The Incident commander could delegate functions to other operational units within the ICS structure, such as the Operations, Logistics, Planning, and Finance/Administration sections (ICAO, 2019). Each of these units plays a crucial role in managing resources and executing specific actions to contain and mitigate the incident.

One of the most important features of the ICS is its "unity of command" approach. This principle ensures that each member of the response team has a single superior, eliminating duplication of orders and reducing the risk of confusion at critical moments. This approach is vital in airport environments, where rapid coordination between different institutions, such as fire, police, medical services, and airport personnel, is essential to control the emergency (FAA, 2020).

## Application of the Incident Command System at Airports

In the airport context, the ICS provides a comprehensive structure for managing incidents involving aircraft, airport facilities or large concentrations of people. According to NFPA 403 (2022), Aircraft Rescue Firefighters must be trained in the

implementation of the ICS, ensuring that all responders are aware of their specific role within the structure and act in a coordinated manner with other teams.

During an airport emergency, the ICS allows the different groups to operate under the same action plan, coordinated through the Incident Commander and his command team. This includes everything from aircraft fire containment to the safe evacuation of passengers and the protection of critical infrastructure, such as fuel depots or air traffic control centers (NFPA 403, 2022). The ability of the ICS to quickly integrate different external institutions is also essential, especially at large airports where the complexity of incidents may require the intervention of additional specialized bodies, such as hazardous materials response units or emergency medical teams (ICAO, 2019).

An example of the effectiveness of ICS in airport emergencies is the crash of Asiana Airlines Flight 214 in 2013, when a Boeing 777 crashed during final approach to San Francisco International Airport. The implementation of the ICS allowed multiple

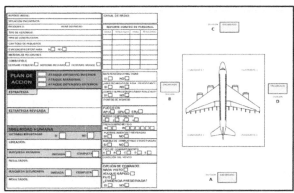

institutions, including Aircraft Rescue Firefighters, local firefighters, medical personnel, and security forces, to work together under one command structure. Thanks to this coordination, passengers were quickly evacuated before the fire consumed much of the aircraft, minimizing the loss of life (NTSB, 2014).

Incident Command System Based Procedures and Protocols

Proper response planning should include specific procedures and protocols based on the ICS. These procedures should be designed to guide immediate action during the first moments of an emergency, ensuring that all available resources are deployed effectively. The ICS states that procedures and plans should be clear and easily accessible to all responders, detailing specific steps such as Incident Command activation, initial situation assessment, and designation of key roles, such as safety, liaison, and public information officers (FAA, 2020).

Response planning should also include mutual aid agreements and the creation of inventories of resources, both available and potentially available, to ensure that all necessary equipment is ready for immediate use. Aircraft Rescue Firefighters should be familiar with these resources and the procedures for requesting and effectively using them during an emergency (NFPA 403, 2022).

## 2.2 Standard Operating Procedures (SOPs)

Standard Operating Procedures (SOPs) are fundamental in airport emergency management and effective response to aircraft-related incidents. These procedures allow the standardization of response actions, ensuring that all members of the aeronautical fire team, as well as external institutions involved, work in a coordinated and efficient manner. The implementation of SOPs is a requirement established by international regulations, such as the National Fire Protection Association (NFPA) 403, the International Civil Aviation Organization (ICAO) and the Federal Aviation Administration (FAA), which highlight the importance of having predefined protocols to manage emergency situations (NFPA 403, 2022; ICAO, 2019; FAA, 2020).

## Definition and Scope of the Standard Operating Procedures SOP's

SOPs are defined as a set of specific instructions outlining the actions to be taken during an aeronautical emergency. These procedures are designed to address a wide range of incidents, which can include everything from aircraft fires and fuel spills to runway accidents and hazardous materials situations. By standardizing the steps to be taken, SOPs ensure that Aircraft Rescue Firefighters can respond quickly and effectively, minimizing human, material and environmental losses.

## TACTICS AND STRATEGIES FOR AIRCRAFT FIREFIGHTING

According to NFPA 403: Standard for Aircraft Rescue and Fire-Fighting Services at Airports, SOPs must be clear, detailed and tailored to the specific characteristics of each airport. Factors such as the number of runways, infrastructure, response capacity and available resources must be taken into account when drafting procedures that are both practical and efficient. Also, procedures should include actions to be taken by other teams and institutions that are part of the response system, such as medical services, security forces and airport operators (NFPA 403, 2022).

### Structure of Standard Operating Procedures

The structure of SOPs varies depending on the type of incident being addressed, but generally speaking, the procedures consist of the following phases:

1. **Alert and Activation of the Emergency Protocol:** This initial phase involves the detection of the incident and the activation of the airport's alarm systems. Once the alarm is activated, the response teams must mobilize in accordance with their assigned duties. It is crucial that Aircraft Rescue Firefighters follow a previously established action plan, minimizing response time (ICAO, 2019).
2. **Initial Incident Assessment:** Once on scene, the team should conduct a rapid assessment of the incident, determining the extent of the fire, immediate hazards, and evacuation needs. This initial assessment is critical to the subsequent allocation of resources and coordination of teams on the ground (FAA, 2020).
3. **Fire Control and Rescue:** In aircraft fires, fire control is the immediate priority. SOPs establish specific steps for the use of equipment such as aircraft rescue and firefighting (ARFF) vehicles and the types of foam or extinguishing agents best suited for each type of fuel present (NFPA 403, 2022). In addition, the procedures include methods of access to aircraft and coordination of rescue operations.

4. **Evacuation of Passengers and Crew:** Procedures should detail how the safe evacuation of aircraft occupants will be accomplished. This phase involves coordination with airport operators and security forces to establish security perimeters and evacuation zones, as well as the implementation of rapid access routes for medical teams (ICAO, 2019).

5. **Damage Assessment and Risk Containment:** Once the main incident is under control, a detailed damage assessment is performed, including verification of the aircraft structure, the condition of the fuel systems, and the possible presence of hazardous materials. SOPs establish the steps to be taken to secure the area, contain spills, and neutralize potential additional hazards (FAA, 2020).

6. **Demobilization and Post-Incident Review:** SOPs should also include protocols for demobilizing equipment, clearing the scene, and conducting a post-incident debriefing, where the strengths and weaknesses of the response are discussed. This review process is essential to improve the effectiveness of future procedures and ensure that lessons learned are implemented (NFPA 1561, 2022).

### Adaptation of SOPs to Airport Infrastructure

Each airport has unique characteristics that must be considered when drafting SOPs. The layout of runways, critical structures, and access points for firefighters are essential elements that determine how operating procedures should be implemented. At airports with a significant volume of air traffic, for example, SOPs should include measures for rapid reallocation of resources in the event that multiple incidents occur simultaneously.

In addition, SOPs must be flexible to accommodate different types of aircraft. As mentioned in NFPA 403, the response to a fire on a wide-body aircraft such as a Boeing 777 is different from that of a smaller aircraft due to the difference in critical access points, fuel systems, and number of passengers on board (NFPA 403, 2022).

## TACTICS AND STRATEGIES FOR AIRCRAFT FIREFIGHTING

This variability in response operations requires that SOPs be specific to each aircraft model operating at the airport.

### SOP-Based Training and Drills

The effectiveness of SOPs depends directly on the training of personnel in their use. Aircraft Rescue Firefighters, as well as collaborating institutions, should be familiar with the procedures through regular training and drills. These practical exercises identify potential failures in the execution of the procedures and provide opportunities for continuous improvement (FAA, 2020).

Emergency drills, which should be conducted regularly in accordance with ICAO and NFPA standards, are vital to assess the ability of the fire team and other emergency services to implement SOPs in a high-pressure environment. In addition, these drills allow procedures to be updated based on changes in airport infrastructure or technological advances (ICAO, 2019).

### Importance of Interinstitutional Coordination in the SOPs

One of the keys to the effectiveness of SOPs is interagency coordination. Aeronautical incidents often involve not only firefighters, but also other institutions, such as emergency medical services, airport police and hazardous materials management brigades. The integration of these entities into SOPs ensures that the response is unified and that all actors work under a single plan of action, which minimizes duplication of effort and reduces the risk of confusion at the incident scene (NFPA 1561, 2022).

Mutual aid agreements with other local or regional emergency institutions should also be part of the SOP, ensuring that additional resources can be deployed quickly when needed. Contingency planning within the procedures ensures that, even in the most complex scenarios, the airport has the necessary human and material resources to manage the situation.

# TACTICS AND STRATEGIES FOR AIRCRAFT FIREFIGHTING

## 2.3 Intervention Protocols

In the context of airport emergency operations, intervention protocols play a crucial role in the coordination and execution of response activities. Protocols are specific guidelines that establish how and when actions should be executed during an incident, as opposed to procedures, which focus on what to do in terms of steps to follow. Clarity in the distinction between procedures and protocols is essential to ensure an effective and coordinated response, minimizing risk and maximizing operational efficiency.

The Incident Command System (ICS), as established by USAID BHA, is a framework that organizes emergency response through a flexible and scalable structure. This allows for efficient and coordinated intervention among the various institutions involved in an aeronautical emergency. The standardization of protocols under the ICS facilitates resource management, assignment of responsibilities and critical decision making in high-pressure situations (USAID BHA, 2021).

### Difference between Procedures and Protocols

The distinction between procedures and protocols is key in the planning and execution of airport emergency response. According to NFPA 403 (2022), procedures are step-by-step instructions that describe specific actions to be taken in specific situations. Procedures are designed to standardize what to do in common incidents, such as aircraft fires, fuel spills or emergency evacuations.

Protocols, on the other hand, are frameworks that guide how those procedures will be executed under different operating conditions. Protocols determine the appropriate time to activate certain procedures and how to adapt those procedures to the changing circumstances of an incident. In other words, while procedures provide specific guidance on the tasks to be performed, protocols provide a strategic framework for decision making during the intervention (NFPA 403, 2022).

## TACTICS AND STRATEGIES FOR AIRCRAFT FIREFIGHTING

In the context of the ICS, protocols are directly related to the efficient use of resources, interagency coordination and the assignment of specific functions within the modular structure of the system. According to USAID BHA (2021), the ICS ensures that protocols are flexible, adapting to the nature of the incident, whether it is an aircraft accident, a hazardous materials situation, or a larger incident requiring the intervention of multiple institutions.

### Intervention Protocols in Aeronautical Emergencies

The ICS establishes that intervention protocols must be clear and allow for the effective coordination of all the actors involved in the emergency. These protocols include the activation of incident command, the designation of key roles, such as the Incident Commander, and coordination between the various institutions, including Aircraft Rescue Firefighters, airport security, medical services, and external institutions (USAID BHA, 2021).

An example of a protocol for intervention in an aeronautical emergency is the Aircraft Fire Control Protocol. This protocol not only includes the procedures for the use of extinguishing agents and the deployment of ARFF (Aircraft Rescue and Firefighting) teams, but also the framework for coordination with the control tower operators, who must ensure the suspension of operations on the affected runway, and with the medical services to establish evacuation areas and treatment of the injured. In this protocol, the Incident commander evaluates the conditions in real time and adjusts the action plan according to the circumstances of the incident (NFPA 403, 2022; FAA, 2020).

Another fundamental aspect of the intervention protocols is the interaction with air traffic control. In an incident involving an aircraft in flight or on an active runway, it is essential that the protocols clearly define the Incident commander's responsibility in coordinating with air traffic control to ensure the safety of other aircraft on approach or takeoff. According to FAA guidelines (2020), it is essential to ensure efficient communication and immediate activation of airport emergency systems.

## Use of Incident Command System Protocols

The ICS, as described by USAID BHA (2021), is an adaptive system that allows for rapid implementation of protocols depending on the severity of the incident. For example, at an airport with multiple runways, protocols may involve closing secondary runways or diverting aircraft to other areas of the airport. This process should be guided by pre-established protocols that ensure that operational decisions are made efficiently, without compromising the safety of other ongoing operations.

In more complex situations, such as hazardous materials incidents aboard an aircraft, intervention protocols should clearly prioritize actions. According to NFPA 472 (2018), handling hazardous materials in an aviation environment requires immediate risk assessment, accurate identification of the material involved, and implementation of mitigation techniques that minimize exposure to both responders and the public. Protocols should integrate not only specific safety procedures for this type of incident, but also coordination with specialized hazardous materials handling units (HAZMAT).

In these scenarios, the ICS facilitates the integration of multiple institutions, ensuring that intervention protocols are executed by the most qualified individuals and units for each task. This centralized command structure minimizes confusion and ensures a unified and efficient response.

## Training and Drills in the Use of Protocols

Effective implementation of intervention protocols cannot be achieved without ongoing training of response personnel. NFPA 403 (2022) states that protocol training should be an integral part of aeronautical firefighter training programs. These trainings should include realistic simulations that allow responders to become familiar with the execution of protocols in emergency situations.

Simulations also allow for the identification of possible deficiencies in existing protocols, which facilitates their revision and updating according to lessons learned. As suggested by USAID BHA (2021), simulation exercises should include the participation of all institutions involved, from emergency services to airport operators, to ensure effective and smooth coordination.

A fundamental aspect is the implementation of drills based on specific incidents that, although rare, can have catastrophic consequences, such as wide-body aircraft fires, fuel spills in sensitive areas or mass evacuations. Protocols in these cases should be tested under conditions that are as realistic as possible to ensure that strategic decisions are made quickly and in a coordinated manner, reducing the margin for error (FAA, 2020).

## 2.4 Guide for airport emergency planning NFPA 424

Emergency planning in the airport environment is a comprehensive and detailed process that requires collaboration between multiple institutions and the use of tools and regulations to ensure adequate preparedness for any type of incident. In this regard, **NFPA 424: Guide for Airport Emergency Planning** is a standard that provides a detailed framework for developing response plans that cover the possible eventualities that could occur at an airport. This guide has become an essential resource for operational safety leaders and airport rescue and firefighting teams around the world (NFPA 424, 2022).

*NFPA 424* establishes guidelines for the creation of an Airport Emergency Plan (AEP), covering essential aspects such as interagency coordination, risk assessment, definition of intervention procedures, and integration of both local and external resources. In this chapter, we will analyze the key components of airport emergency planning according to *NFPA 424*, exploring how airport emergency response and management teams apply this standard to ensure an effective response.

## Risk and Resource Assessment

One of the first steps defined by *NFPA 424* in emergency planning is risk assessment. This process involves a detailed identification of all hazards that could affect an airport, such as aircraft fires, runway accidents, fuel spills or hazardous materials emergencies. The risk assessment should also consider airport infrastructure, air traffic volume, geographical features of the environment, and the responsiveness of local resources (NFPA 424, 2022).

Risk analysis allows airport security managers to prioritize critical areas and define the necessary mitigation strategies. As a safety leader, it is essential to coordinate this analysis with all institutions involved in emergency response, including local authorities, Aircraft Rescue Firefighters, airport police and emergency medical services. According to the guidance, the assessment of available resources is also critical to determine the airport's operational capabilities and external resources that may be required in the event of a major emergency (USAID BHA, 2021).

## Inter-institutional Coordination and Role Assignment

*NFPA 424* stresses the importance of interagency coordination in airport emergency planning. Since incidents at an airport involve multiple players, from security personnel and firefighters to air traffic controllers and medical teams, the guidance states that it is crucial to define specific roles and responsibilities for each agency involved in the response (NFPA 424, 2022). The Incident Command System (ICS), used as an international standard and promoted by USAID BHA, is the recommended structure for coordinating these activities, assigning clear roles under a unified command (USAID BHA, 2021).

In this phase, communication protocols are established between all entities to ensure that information flows efficiently and accurately during the response. *NFPA 424* recommends periodic meetings between the institutions involved to ensure that all actors are aligned with established procedures and protocols. This coordination also allows for the identification of additional resources that may be needed during an emergency, such as specialized rescue teams or hazardous materials units (NFPA 1561, 2022).

## Operating Procedures and Intervention Protocols

A key aspect of airport emergency planning is the definition of standard operating procedures (SOPs) and intervention protocols. As mentioned in previous chapters, procedures are detailed sequences of steps to be followed during an incident, while protocols guide decision-making on when and how to execute those procedures. *NFPA 424* details how these should be tailored to the specifics of each airport and its specific operations.

| Bomberos Aeronáuticos Cali Manual de procedimientos operativos | Procedimiento operativo No. P-17 | Fecha de elaboración: 27/Marzo/2015 | Páginas: 1 de 1 | Nombre del procedimiento: Respuesta a Emergencias en B-777ER |
|---|---|---|---|---|
| Propósito: Conducir las de manera eficaz las operaciones de Emergencia en la Aeronave de mayor envergadura que aterriza en el Aeropuerto Albonar de Cali B-777ER | | | | Responsable: Oficial de servicio |

Calculo de Área Critica Practica en el B-777ER:

61.73m

Área Critica Teórica 1.152 m

5.86 m

Área Critica Practica 772 m

For example, SOPs for an aircraft fire should include not only fire control methods, but also aircraft access routes, evacuation points, and medical support systems. Protocols, on the other hand, should define operational priorities, such as protection of critical areas and coordination with airport personnel to suspend operations on nearby runways (NFPA 403, 2022). These actions should be integrated into the Airport Emergency Plan and be subject to drills and practical exercises to ensure that teams are prepared to act quickly and accurately.

### Drills and Training

*NFPA 424* highlights the importance of drills as part of the airport emergency planning process. These exercises allow the effectiveness of established procedures and protocols to be tested, identify possible gaps in the response and reinforce coordination between the different institutions involved. The drills also provide personnel with the opportunity to familiarize themselves with the resources and equipment available, as well as with the specific characteristics of the airport.

According to USAID BHA guidelines, drills should include realistic scenarios covering a variety of possible emergencies, from aircraft fires to mass evacuations due to terrorist threats. In addition, these exercises should involve not only aeronautical fire personnel, but also external institutions, such as medical services and police, to ensure a comprehensive and coordinated response (USAID BHA, 2021).

### Community Integration and Mutual Aid

Finally, *NFPA 424* addresses the importance of integrating community and mutual aid agreements into the airport emergency plan. Airports often rely on the resources of nearby communities, such as local emergency services, and it is essential that these stakeholders are integrated into planning. *NFPA 424* recommends that airports establish formal mutual aid agreements with outside institutions that can provide additional support in the event of a major incident (IFSTA, 2019).

These agreements not only ensure the availability of additional resources, but also facilitate the implementation of regionally coordinated emergency operations. Collaboration with the community also includes educational campaigns to raise public awareness of safety and evacuation procedures in the event of an airport emergency.

## 2.5 Operational Planning - The "P" in Planning

Operational planning is an essential part of the Incident Command System (ICS) that ensures that all actions during an emergency are coordinated, effective and adapted to the evolution of the incident. Within the framework of airport emergency management, the planning process is particularly critical, as the complexity of airports and the various variables involved in an incident require a structured and proactive approach.

The "P" concept of planning, developed and used within the ICS, describes a continuous cycle that guides responders from the initial assessment of the situation through the implementation and evaluation of actions taken. According to *the National Incident Command System* (NIMS) *Guidance*, operational planning is a key function that ensures the creation of well-defined action plans consistent with the strategic objectives established at the onset of the incident (NIMS, 2021)(NIMS-incident-complexity).

### Planning "P" Cycle

The "P" cycle of planning begins with the preparedness phase and extends through the Incident Action Plan (IAP) assessment and adjustment phase. Throughout this cycle, the leadership of the Incident commander and the planning teams is crucial to efficiently manage resources and ensure the safety of response personnel. The planning cycle is structured in five interrelated phases:

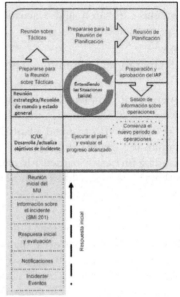

1. **Understand the Situation**: In this phase, initial incident data is collected and analyzed to form a clear picture of what is occurring. This includes information on the location of the incident, immediate hazards, available resources, and weather conditions. This phase is critical to making informed decisions that guide the rest of the planning cycle. As FEMA (2010) explains, accurate and timely data collection is essential for effective airport emergency response (FEMA_Handbook_2010).

2. **Establish Objectives and Strategies**: From the information obtained, the planning team should formulate clear objectives and strategies that define the actions to be taken. These objectives should be specific, measurable, achievable, relevant and time-bound (SMART), aligned with the Incident Commander's guidelines (SCI, 2021)(Manual_SCI_2014_OFDA).

3. **Development of the Incident Action Plan (IAP):** Once the objectives have been defined, the IAP is developed, which details the specific tactics that will be used to achieve those objectives. This plan should include resource allocations, access routes, critical control points and responsibilities for each team involved. Effective IAP planning, as highlighted by the *SCI Field Manual* (2014), is an essential tool for all stakeholders to be aligned and prepared to execute their roles during the incident (Manual_SCI_2014_OFDA) (NIMS_AppendixB).

4. **Prepare and Disseminate the IAP:** After developing the IAP, it is crucial to communicate the plan to everyone involved in the incident. Clear dissemination of the IAP ensures that each team knows its role and has access to the necessary resources. In addition, briefings should be established so that all responders are aligned and any changes in incident conditions are effectively incorporated into the plan.

5. **Execute, Evaluate and Review the IAP:** The final phase of the cycle consists of the execution of the IAP and its subsequent evaluation. During execution, it is important to monitor the development of the incident and make real-time adjustments if necessary. Once the emergency is under control, a formal review of the IAP should be conducted, identifying areas of improvement for future incidents (NIMS, 2021) (NIMS-incident-complexity).

**Importance of Airport Emergency Planning**

In an airport environment, operational planning must not only be detailed, but also highly flexible to adapt to the different types of incidents that can occur. The diversity of emergencies at an airport-such as aircraft fires, fuel spills, and hazardous materials situations-requires that response plans consider every variable and prepare teams for complex scenarios. According to the *ICS Manual* (2014), proper planning must take into account the unique characteristics of airports, such as proximity to fuel depots, high passenger density, and critical infrastructure (ICS, 2014)(Manual_SCI_2014_OFDA)(Manual_FEMA_2010).

In addition, operational planning at airports must include coordination with multiple institutions and key players, such as Aircraft Rescue Firefighters, medical services, air traffic controllers and security forces. Each of these players has a critical role to play in the execution of emergency plans, and clear and continuous communication is essential to ensure an effective and safe response.

## Planning Tools

Among the most commonly used tools in operational planning are ICS forms, such as the *ICS Form 201*, which allows the Incident Commander to perform an initial summary of the incident and provide a clear outline for the development of the IAP (FEMA, 2010)(Manual_FEMA_2010). These forms help standardize planning and ensure that all relevant information is considered and distributed effectively.

Another key tool is the use of drills and practical exercises to test the effectiveness of action plans. These exercises help identify gaps in planning and improve long-term response strategies.

## 2.6 Designing an Incident Action Plan (IAP)

In the field of airport emergencies, proper planning is essential to ensure an efficient and safe response to incidents involving aircraft. The Incident Action Plan (IAP) is a crucial component in emergency management, as it provides structured guidance for decision making, resource coordination and execution of tactics that safeguard the lives of people and infrastructure. Throughout my years of experience as an aeronautical firefighter, I have observed how the effective implementation of an IAP can make the difference between a successful response and a catastrophic outcome. In this article, we will examine the key components of an IAP and their relevance to aeronautical emergencies, based on National Fire Protection Association (NFPA), USAID BHA, IFSTA and FEMA regulations.

## The AIP Concept in the Incident Command System (ICS)

The Incident Command System (ICS), developed by FEMA and adopted internationally, is the organizational structure that facilitates the effective management of any type of emergency, including those involving aircraft. Within this framework, the IAP is configured as the central document that coordinates all tactical and strategic actions. According to the USAID BHA ICS Manual (2014), the IAP should include clear objectives, strategies to achieve them, and specific tactics that adapt to changing incident conditions. This plan, in addition to structuring operations, also facilitates communication between the different actors involved, ensuring that everyone works under the same operational scheme.

The flexibility of the IAP allows it to adjust to the scale of the incident, from an uncomplicated emergency landing to a multi-casualty accident. This adaptability is one of the most important aspects of the ICS, as each aviation emergency presents unique challenges that require a customized approach (FEMA, 2010).

It is necessary to clarify that there are 2 types of AIP (Mental and Written).

## Mental

We must always plan, even if we are in the initial phase (understanding the situation), in this phase, the AIP must be mental, this requires the fire officer to have clear criteria, master the standard operating procedures, mental agility and ability to transmit to his subordinates what he has planned through a Briefing.

# TACTICS AND STRATEGIES FOR AIRCRAFT FIREFIGHTING

**Written**

At a later stage, when we cannot resolve the situation in the initial phase (the first 4 hours), we have to think about an incident that has escalated, it is essential to plan in writing through the form SCI 202 (Incident Action Plan), this action ensures that everything is clear at the time of launching the operational periods.

> *"The AIP is the score that the incident commander leads for his musicians (response personnel) to implement to resolve the situation."*

**Key components of the AIP**

An effective IAP must contain several essential elements that ensure efficient execution of operations. These include:

1. **SMART Objectives:** Objectives should follow the SMART (Specific, Measurable, Achievable, Relevant and Time-bound) criteria. This approach ensures that objectives provide clear and measurable guidance to the response team (FEMA, 2010) and should be written in the *infinitive*.
   o Example: "Evacuate 30 passengers from the aircraft within 15 minutes".
2. **Strategies:** Strategies are the general guidelines that guide action toward the objectives. They should be written in the *simple present tense* to provide clear and direct guidance to the teams involved.
   o Example: "I send three rescue teams to the highest risk areas inside the aircraft."
3. **Tactics:** Tactics are the specific actions being executed to carry out the strategies. They are written in the *gerund* to highlight their ongoing execution.
   o Example: "Using thermal cameras to locate passengers in the cabin and using rapid evacuation stretchers."
4. **Resources and Logistics:** An IAP should also include a detailed list of available resources, from firefighting vehicles

to first aid equipment and containment materials. In addition, logistics play a crucial role in ensuring that all equipment reaches critical areas without delay.

### Implementation of the AIP in Aircraft Incidents

A typical example of the implementation of an IAP in an aircraft emergency could be an emergency landing with a landing gear fire. Upon receiving notification of the incident, the Incident commander would activate the ICS, establishing a clear line of command and activating the corresponding AIP.

1. **Objective:** Evacuate all passengers from inside the aircraft in less than 10 minutes.
2. **Strategy:** "I send two rescue teams inside the aircraft equipped to do primary search".
3. **Tactic:** "Using thermographic cameras to perform technological research."

In this scenario, the IAP would be monitored in real time, with adjustments made if the aircraft presents additional hazards that complicate evacuation. The flexibility of the IAP allows these changes to be implemented quickly, ensuring that the overall objectives remain achievable.

### Training and Drills

One of the best practices in the implementation of an IAP is to conduct regular tabletop simulations and drills. These exercises allow aeronautical fire crews and other responders to become familiar with the IAP and to refine its execution in real-world situations. According to NFPA 403 (2022), training and drills based on aeronautical emergency scenarios are essential to ensure that all players are prepared to respond efficiently.

## TACTICS AND STRATEGIES FOR AIRCRAFT FIREFIGHTING

Drills should include all elements of the EPI, from ICS activation to coordination with external institutions, such as medical services and air traffic controllers. In addition, these drills provide an opportunity to review and improve existing IAPs, ensuring that they conform to the changing realities of the airport environment (NFPA 424, 2022).

### SMART Objectives in Emergency Planning

IAP objectives must meet the SMART criteria, a model that ensures that the objectives are:

- Specific: They should describe precisely what is intended to be achieved.
- Measurable: They must be quantifiable to determine their success or failure.
- Achievable: They must be realistic and within the capabilities of the response team.
- Relevant: They must have a direct impact on the mitigation of the incident.
- Time-bound: They must be defined in a clear and limited period of time.

This SMART approach ensures that objectives provide clear and achievable direction for the response team. Below is an example of an objective written under the SMART model:

- **Objective**: Rescue the 20 victims from the aircraft in less than 20 minutes.

In this example, the objective is specific (rescue victims), measurable (20 victims), achievable (within the capabilities of the rescue team), relevant (save lives) and with a clear time limit (less than 20 minutes).

## TACTICS AND STRATEGIES FOR AIRCRAFT FIREFIGHTING

### Aeronautical Emergency Response Strategies and Tactics

The strategy is the overall approach taken to achieve the IAP objectives, while the tactics are the specific actions that the team executes to accomplish the strategy. Strategies are written in the **simple present tense**, while tactics are written in the **gerund**, as they describe ongoing actions. This format ensures clarity and facilitates the orderly execution of activities during the incident.

Example 1: Fire in an aircraft after an emergency landing.

- **Objective**: Extinguish the fire in the aircraft (interior and exterior) in less than 12 minutes and evacuate the passengers without fatalities.
- **Strategy**: I implement the fast attack command mode with specialized extinguishing and rescue teams.
- **Tactical**: Using AFFF (aqueous film-forming foam) foam with boom (bumper) turrets and thermal cameras to locate critical fire points, while coordinating safe evacuation routes.

In this example, the strategy provides clear guidance on the general approach to the operation (fast attack mode), and the tactic specifies the resources and methods to be used (AFFF foam and thermal cameras).

Example 2: Landing gear detachment on the runway

- **Objective**: Remove the landing gear wreckage within 15 minutes to reopen the runway to normal operations.
- **Strategy**: I deploy a resources team and heavy machinery for aircraft removal.
- **Tactical**: Using specialized cranes, cleaning the runway with suction equipment and ensuring that there are no fuel spills.

## TACTICS AND STRATEGIES FOR AIRCRAFT FIREFIGHTING

### Key phases of the AIP

The IAP is structured in key phases, each with objectives, strategies and tactics that ensure a smooth and coordinated response. According to the *ICS Manual* (USAID BHA, 2014), the phases of the IAP should be constantly monitored and adjusted to adapt to the evolution of the incident.

1. **Initial Preparedness Phase**: Involves notification of the incident, initial assessment of the situation and activation of the Incident Command System (ICS). Initial objectives and strategies to control the incident are established in this phase.
   - **Objective**: Activate the ICS within 5 minutes of incident notification.
   - **Strategy**: Coordinated the activation of command units and the mobilization of first response teams.
   - **Tactical**: Using emergency communication channels, notifying air and ground teams, and assigning roles to sector commanders.
2. **Field Operations Phase**: Once the ICS is established, field operations should focus on incident containment, responder safety and evacuation of those affected.
   - **Objective**: Evacuate injured passengers to the victim concentration area (VCA) in less than 15 minutes.
   - **Strategy**: I coordinate evacuation efforts with airport security brigades.
   - **Tactical**: Using stretchers and following defined safe routes to the ACV.
3. **Containment and Resolution Phase**: This phase is about ensuring total control of the incident, either by extinguishing the fire, mitigating the impact of hazardous substance spills, or any other critical action needed.
   - **Objective**: Control the fuel spill within 30 minutes to prevent contamination of water sources.

## TACTICS AND STRATEGIES FOR AIRCRAFT FIREFIGHTING

- o **Strategy**: I arrange for a specialized hazardous materials handling team to contain and confine the spill.
- o **Tactical**: Using absorbent barriers, performing capping and ensuring ventilation of the affected area.

## AIP Tools: Forms and Documentation

The design of the IAP requires the use of standardized documentation tools to facilitate incident planning and monitoring. One of the most relevant documents in the IAP structure is the **SCI Form 202**, which defines the operational and strategic objectives of the incident. This form, recommended by the *National ICS Guide* and FEMA, provides a standardized platform for the Incident commander to clearly communicate objectives to the entire team (FEMA, 2010) (Manual_FEMA_2010).

In addition, it is essential to use other forms such as SCI 204 (Assignment Checklist) and SCI 206 (Medical Plan) to ensure that all aspects of the incident, from resource allocation to medical safety, are considered in the IAP (NIMS-incident-complexity...)(Manual_FEMA_2010).

## API Evaluation and Adjustment

One of the strengths of the ICS is its flexibility to adapt to the evolution of an incident. The IAP must be constantly monitored and adjusted based on the changing circumstances of the incident. This process of continuous adjustment is essential to ensure that the objectives initially established remain achievable and that strategies and tactics remain aligned with the current incident situation.

- • **Objective**: Re-evaluate the effectiveness of firefighting tactics every 10 minutes.

- **Strategy**: I maintain constant monitoring of the fire through updated situation reports.
- **Tactical**: Using real-time communication systems, soliciting feedback from team leaders on the progress of the operation.

### 2.7 Status, Classification and Categorization of Resources

In any airport emergency, especially those involving aircraft fires, proper management of resources is critical to ensure an effective response. Resources range from specialized personnel and firefighting equipment to vehicles, medical supplies, and rescue tools. According to *Federal Emergency Management Agency* (FEMA) and USAID BHA guidelines, in order for these resources to be mobilized and utilized efficiently, it is essential to establish their status, classification and typing (FEMA, 2010). This process not only facilitates the rapid allocation of resources, but also ensures that the equipment deployed is appropriate for the type of incident and environmental conditions.

### The State of Resources

The status of resources refers to their immediate availability for deployment in an emergency. Resources can be classified into three main states according to FEMA's National Incident Management System (NIMS) guidance: "available," "assigned," and "out of service." Each status has implications on the ability of the response team to utilize those resources at any given time.

## TACTICS AND STRATEGIES FOR AIRCRAFT FIREFIGHTING

- **Available**: Resources that are ready to be mobilized immediately. For example, an ARFF firefighting vehicle fully loaded with AFFF foam and in perfect condition is an "available" resource to intervene in an aircraft fire.

- **Assigned**: Resources that are already committed to responding to an incident. In this state, a fire crew that has already been deployed to a runway where the incident occurred would be considered "assigned," meaning that it is

not available for use in other areas of the airport until it is released from its current assignment.
- **Unavailable**: Resources that, for technical or maintenance reasons, cannot be used in the incident response. According

to FEMA, maintaining an updated inventory of the status of resources is essential to ensure that equipment is in optimal condition to intervene in a timely manner (FEMA, 2010).

Inadequate management of resource status can lead to critical delays during an emergency. For example, in a situation where firefighting equipment or rescue vehicles are "out of service" without commanders being aware, it could create confusion and slow down the intervention.

### Classification of Resources

Resource classification refers to the categorization of equipment, personnel, and materials based on their specific capabilities and functions within the incident. According to FEMA and USAID BHA regulations, resources should be organized into different categories to facilitate their rapid and efficient mobilization (USAID BHA, 2021). In the context of aviation emergencies, the classification of resources can follow several lines, including:

1. **Human Resources**: Aircraft Rescue Firefighters, paramedics, aeronautical engineers, safety teams and firefighting vehicle operators.
2. **Fire Fighting Vehicles and Equipment**: ARFF fire suppression vehicles are classified resources based on their ability to carry water, foam, or chemical agents. For example, an ARFF vehicle capable of deploying 4500

gallons of AFFF foam is suitable for a large aircraft incident, while a smaller vehicle may be used for smaller incidents.

3. **Specialized Equipment**: Thermal cameras for searching for people in the fuselage, respiratory protection equipment, fuselage cutters and stretchers for rapid evacuation are examples of resources that should be classified according to their functionality.

4. **Medical Supplies**: These include first aid supplies, automatic defibrillators (AEDs), trauma kits, and medevac vehicles. Medical resources should be classified according to their ability to treat critical injuries and stabilize the injured prior to transport to nearby hospitals.

**Importance of Efficient Resource Management**

Efficient resource management is key to the success of any emergency operation. According to *National Fire Protection Association* (NFPA) regulations, each airport must maintain an up-to-date inventory of its resources, classify them and type them appropriately so that they are ready to be deployed at a moment's notice (NFPA 424, 2022). In addition, resource tracking systems allow incident commanders to make informed decisions about equipment allocation, ensuring that the most appropriate resources reach critical areas in the shortest possible time.

The use of advanced technologies, such as real-time resource management systems, allows for greater accuracy in monitoring their status and location. These tools, as mentioned by USAID BHA (2021), facilitate the automatic updating of inventories and ensure that the Incident Commander and his team have immediate access to critical information on available and assigned resources.

**Class and Type of Resources in Emergency Management: A FEMA and USAID BHA-Based Approach.**

The correct classification and classification of resources is a fundamental aspect of emergency management. This process ensures that the equipment and materials needed to respond to an incident are available, mobilized quickly and used efficiently. Classification and typing of resources are standardized practices that allow incident commanders and response institutions to know what type of capabilities they have available and how they can be integrated into the Incident Command System (ICS). In this context, typing resources according to *Federal Emergency Management Agency* (FEMA) and USAID BHA guidelines is crucial to ensure interoperability between institutions and a rapid and effective response.

**Resource Class**

The class of a resource refers to its general categorization according to its functionality or purpose within emergency response. Broadly speaking, resources can be classified into three main classes:

1.  **Human Resources**: Include firefighters, paramedics, security personnel, specialized technicians and other human resources who play operational or support roles in the response to an incident.
2.  **Material Resources**: These include all types of equipment, from specialized vehicles, such as ARFF (Aircraft Rescue and Fire Fighting) vehicles, to rescue tools, such as thermal cameras, rapid evacuation stretchers and fuselage cutters.
3.  **Medical and Logistical Supplies**: These include emergency medical supplies, communication systems, extinguishing resources (such as AFFF foam), and personal protective equipment (PPE), among others.

These classes of resources must be categorized and managed efficiently to ensure their availability at the right time and optimize critical incident response (FEMA, 2010).

## TACTICS AND STRATEGIES FOR AIRCRAFT FIREFIGHTING

### Classification of Resources

Resource typing is a step beyond classification, as it involves a detailed standardization of the capabilities and performance of each resource. Under FEMA regulations, resources are typed according to their ability to handle incidents of different magnitudes. The purpose of typing is to ensure that the resources being mobilized meet a minimum performance standard and can be effectively deployed based on the type and size of the incident.

FEMA and USAID BHA divide resources into types, with **Type 1** representing the highest level of capability and **Type 4** representing the lowest. This system allows incident commanders and partner agencies to quickly identify the resources best suited to the nature and severity of the emergency.

1. **Type 1**: Resources with the highest capacity and performance. For example, a Type 1 ARFF firefighting vehicle would be capable of deploying large quantities of extinguishing agents, such as AFFF foam, to fight large aircraft fires. These resources are essential in complex incidents, such as the crash of a wide-body aircraft with multiple casualties.
2. **Type 2**: Resources with moderate capabilities. A Type 2 ARFF vehicle may be used on minor fires or in situations where large-scale intervention is not required, such as a small aircraft fire at a regional airport.
3. **Type 3 and Type 4**: Resources with more limited capabilities, generally used in smaller scale incidents or as additional support in larger emergencies. These resources could include smaller extinguishing vehicles, basic respiratory protection equipment or first responder medical supplies.

This typing system is critical for interoperability between agencies during major incidents that require the mobilization of external resources or resources from different jurisdictional levels. According to USAID BHA (2021), standardized typing allows institutions collaborating under mutual aid agreements to provide resources efficiently and according to the specific needs of the incident.

### Example of Typing in Aeronautical Emergencies

In the context of an aeronautical emergency, such as a large aircraft accident, resource typing plays a crucial role in ensuring that the appropriate teams are mobilized quickly. An incident of this magnitude might require the mobilization of **Type 1** ARFF vehicles, equipped with large quantities of foam and extinguishing agents to deal with flames and possible fuel explosions.

- **Type 1 Resource**: An ARFF vehicle capable of deploying more than 4,500 gallons of AFFF foam, required for large-scale incidents.
- **Type 2 Resource**: A team specialized in rescue and evacuation of people trapped in the aircraft, equipped with thermal cameras and fuselage cutters.
- **Type 3 Resource**: A first aid team that provides basic medical care at the scene of an accident prior to the arrival of higher capacity paramedics.

The correct classification and mobilization of these resources ensures that the incident is managed efficiently and that the response teams can act according to the severity of the situation.

### Importance of Resource Typing

Resource typing not only ensures that the appropriate resources are used effectively during an incident, but also facilitates interoperability between different institutions, both locally and nationally. In large-scale emergencies, such as natural disasters or complex aircraft crashes, it is common to need the support of external institutions. Standardized typing allows these institutions to mobilize resources that meet the requirements of the incident without generating confusion or duplicating efforts (USAID BHA, 2021).

For example, if an airport is faced with an emergency that exceeds its capabilities, it can request additional resources through mutual aid agreements. By using a typing system, external institutions can quickly identify and provide the necessary resources, ensuring that they meet incident-specific standards and requirements.

## 2.8 Standby Levels and Command Modes

In emergency response, especially in the airport environment, standby levels and command modes are fundamental aspects that determine the effectiveness of the intervention. These concepts are deeply embedded in the Incident Command System (ICS), providing a flexible framework that adapts to the severity of the incident and available resources. Both standby levels and command modes help Aircraft Rescue Firefighters and responders organize and act in a coordinated manner. In this chapter, we will explore how these concepts are applied, based on *National Fire Protection Association* (NFPA), *International Civil Aviation Organization (ICAO), Federal Aviation Administration* (FAA) regulations and best practices described in the book *Fire Command* by Alan Brunacini (2002).

### Waiting Levels in Airport Emergencies

Standby levels refer to the different stages of preparedness and mobilization of response resources before an active intervention is initiated. In the context of airport emergencies, it is essential that response teams adopt a tiered approach, aligned with potential risk scenarios. According to NFPA 403 (2022), standby levels are a key tool to keep teams on alert without compromising operational efficiency.

# TACTICS AND STRATEGIES FOR AIRCRAFT FIREFIGHTING

## Waiting Levels according to the Severity of the Incident

The classification of waiting levels may vary according to the type of airport and the available infrastructure, but the following hierarchy is used:

1. **Level 1 (Low):** Corresponds to situations where the emergency has not yet materialized, but response teams must be ready (readiness) to act if the situation changes. For example, an aircraft reporting minor problems during flight could activate a low standby level. At this level, firefighting and rescue vehicles will be on standby without displacement (NFPA 403, 2022).

2. **Level 2 (Moderate):** At this level, the emergency has materialized or an imminent risk exists. Firefighting, rescue and other resources must be fully ready to mobilize. An example might be an aircraft making an emergency landing due to a serious technical failure. In this case, response personnel are positioned near the expected point of impact, with firefighting and rescue resources already deployed.

3. **Level 3 (High):** This level corresponds to active emergencies in progress, such as a plane crash or aircraft fire. Extinguishing and rescue teams are fully mobilized and in operation. According to Brunacini (2002), at this level coordination between teams is vital, and a strong, centralized command is required to ensure that resources are optimally utilized.

Standby levels are not only useful for maintaining team readiness, but also allow the Incident Commander to adjust resource mobilization as the emergency evolves. This flexibility is crucial at airports, where emergencies can vary in complexity and require different degrees of response (NFPA 1561, 2022).

## TACTICS AND STRATEGIES FOR AIRCRAFT FIREFIGHTING

### Command Modes

Command mode refers to how the Incident commander organizes and directs the response to an emergency. According to Alan Brunacini in *Fire Command* (2002), command modes allow the leader to adjust the command structure based on incident conditions and available resources. Command modes also ensure that operations remain organized, effective and safe.

### Command Modes: Fast Attack Mode, Steady Mode and Transitional Mode in Emergency Management

In emergency response, especially those involving aircraft, command modes are essential for efficient decision making and organization of resources. Based on Alan Brunacini's *Fire Command* and NFPA regulations, three key command modes can be identified in incident management: **rapid attack, fixed mode**, and **transitional mode**. Each of these modes provides a response strategy adaptable to the situation and phase of the incident, ensuring that resources are utilized effectively and safely.

### Fast Attack Mode

The **rapid attack mode** is an immediate response strategy, usually implemented by the first officer to arrive at the incident scene. This mode is used in situations where the incident commander can jump directly into action to stabilize the emergency. According to Brunacini, rapid attack is critical when immediate intervention can be made to control the incident before it escalates (Brunacini, 2002).

## TACTICS AND STRATEGIES FOR AIRCRAFT FIREFIGHTING

In the context of an aircraft fire, the rapid attack mode involves an immediate response to contain the fire before it spreads to the airframe or nearby fuel areas. Firefighting vehicles, such as ARFFs (Aircraft Rescue and Firefighting), are quickly positioned to apply AFFF foam and mitigate the fire while more complex command lines are established.

The key to rapid attack is the commander's ability to make immediate decisions and coordinate resources dynamically. In this mode, the commander remains directly involved in operations until the incident stabilizes or the situation requires a more comprehensive and planned approach (NFPA 1561, 2022).

### Fixed Mode

The **fixed mode**, also known as "stationary command mode," is the next step when the incident is partially stabilized, but still requires coordinated intervention on a larger scale. In this mode, the commander is established at a fixed command post outside the danger zone, from where he/she can manage resources and tactical operations in a more controlled manner (Brunacini, 2002).

This mode is essential in prolonged incidents, where the commander needs to stay away from active operations to focus on strategic coordination. In an airport emergency scenario, the fixed mode could be implemented once the aircraft fire is under control, but the rescue and evacuation operation is still ongoing. From the fixed command post, the commander can monitor the progress of the incident, assign additional resources and coordinate with other institutions, such as medical and security services.

The use of fixed mode ensures that decisions are made with a broad perspective of the incident, allowing the commander to anticipate problems and adjust strategies more effectively.

## TACTICS AND STRATEGIES FOR AIRCRAFT FIREFIGHTING

### Transitional Mode

**Transitional mode** is an intermediate strategy that allows the incident commander to switch between rapid attack and stationary command as the incident evolves. This mode is used when an incident begins with a fast attack, but the situation becomes more complicated or prolonged, requiring a transition to a more organized and stationary command.

In aircraft incidents, transitional mode is common when a seemingly controllable situation, such as a small fire on the runway, develops into a more complex incident involving multiple vehicles and rescue teams. According to NFPA recommendations and Brunacini's principles, the incident commander must be able to adapt quickly to these changes, moving from the field to a more strategic supervisory position when necessary (NFPA 1561, 2022; Brunacini, 2002).

The shift to transitional mode allows the commander to maintain close control during the critical initial phases of the incident, but also provides the flexibility to move to a more strategic approach once operations are underway. This is essential in aviation emergencies, where speed and flexibility are key to saving lives and minimizing damage.

### 2.9 Personnel Counting System

In aeronautical emergency operations, proper personnel management is essential to ensure an efficient and safe response. The Personnel Counting System (PCS) is a critical tool that allows incident commanders to keep an accurate record of all those involved in the operation. This system ensures not only the location and control of personnel, but also effective coordination between the different teams, avoiding duplication and ensuring that safety procedures are followed. Based on the *National Fire Protection Association* (NFPA) regulations, the Incident Command System (ICS) and the best practices of USAID BHA, ICAO, FAA and IFSTA, we will examine the importance and key components of the PCS in emergency management.

## Importance of the Personnel Counting System

The main objective of the CPS is to ensure the safety of responders. In emergencies involving aircraft, where conditions are highly dangerous, such as fires, fuel spills or collisions, maintaining tight control of personnel is essential to prevent anyone from being trapped or in danger without the command's knowledge. According to NFPA 1500 (2022), personnel monitoring through the SCP significantly reduces the risk of loss of life among firefighters and other responders.

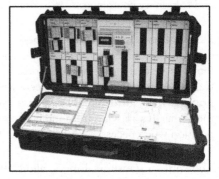

In addition to ensuring safety, the SCP also improves operational efficiency. By knowing exactly how many manpower resources are available and where they are located, the Incident Commander can make informed decisions on tasking. This ensures that the right teams are directed to critical areas, maximizing the effectiveness of the operation and minimizing the risk of miscoordination.

The *Incident Command System Field Manual* (USAID BHA, 2021) stresses the importance of the PCS as a tool for managing both human and material resources during complex emergencies. Accurate personnel counts also facilitate the transition between different command modes, such as rapid attack, fixed mode, or transitional mode, ensuring that all responders are aware of changes and aligned with the objectives of the Incident Action Plan (IAP).

## TACTICS AND STRATEGIES FOR AIRCRAFT FIREFIGHTING

## Components of the Personnel Counting System

An effective CPS must include several key elements to ensure its proper functioning in aviation emergencies. These elements are designed to provide continuous, up-to-date monitoring of the location and status of all team members.

1. **Check In and Check Out**: This is the central component of the CPS, where each responder must check in upon arrival at the incident scene and upon departure. The log allows the Incident commander to keep an up-to-date count of how many people are active in the operation at any given time. According to NFPA 1561 (2022), the system must be robust enough to include not only fire personnel, but also medical, security and logistics teams.

2. **Task Assignment**: The SCP should be linked to the command and control structure of the ICS. Each team member should be clearly assigned to a specific unit or task, and this information should be constantly updated. This component ensures that there is no duplication of effort and that each team is working according to the established IAP (Brunacini, 2002).

3. **Personnel Identification System**: Using tools such as identification cards or electronic devices is an NFPA recommended practice to improve the accuracy of the count. Electronic systems, such as chips, allow the Incident commander to monitor the real-time location of personnel within the incident area, which is especially useful in complex or large-scale situations (NFPA 1500, 2022).

4. **Communication System**: An effective CPS must be closely linked to emergency communication systems. This ensures that any change in personnel status, such as the need to evacuate or reassign a team, can be immediately communicated to the members involved. The integration of radio communications and real-time control systems facilitates greater responsiveness and operational adjustment (USAID BHA, 2021).

## TACTICS AND STRATEGIES FOR AIRCRAFT FIREFIGHTING

## Implementation of the CPS in Aeronautical Emergencies

In the context of an emergency involving aircraft, the CPS is activated from the moment aeronautical fire and rescue teams arrive at the scene of the incident. In a situation such as an emergency landing with engine fire, each firefighter must check in and be assigned to a specific task, such as  extinguishing the fire or evacuating passengers.

A concrete example of the effective use of PCS in aviation emergencies is the Asiana Airlines Flight 214 accident in 2013, where proper implementation of personnel headcount allowed commanders to maintain control of teams during the rescue operation. Effective coordination and tracking of personnel reduced the initial chaos and ensured that teams were assigned to the areas of greatest need (NTSB, 2014).

In addition, the PCS is vital in prolonged situations where multiple shifts of personnel are involved. In these cases, the system must manage the proper relief of teams, ensuring that operations continue without interruption and that work time limits are not exceeded, as recommended by NFPA 1584 on the management of physical effort in emergencies.

## Challenges and Best Practices

Despite its importance, the implementation of the PCS is not without its challenges. One of the main problems is the reluctance of personnel to strictly adhere to logging procedures. According to Alan Brunacini's *Fire Command*, commanders must continually emphasize the importance of following these protocols as a matter of personal and operational safety (Brunacini, 2002).

Another complication is the lack of integration between manual and electronic counting systems. NFPA regulations suggest that airports adopt hybrid systems, where manual check-in is complemented by advanced electronic systems that provide an additional layer of security and accuracy in personnel counting.

To overcome these challenges, ongoing training of personnel in the use of the PCS is recommended, as well as conducting regular drills where the effectiveness of the system is tested in simulated emergency situations (NFPA 1561, 2022). The feedback obtained from these exercises can be invaluable in adjusting and improving the system.

## Conclusion

The Incident Command System provides an essential framework for emergency management in the airport environment. Its ability to structure and coordinate the response of multiple institutions, together with its focus on clear delegation of responsibilities and unification of command, makes it an indispensable tool for Aircraft Rescue Firefighters. Successful ICS implementation depends not only on detailed and consistent planning, but also on continuous training of personnel, ensuring that they are prepared to respond to any type of incident quickly and effectively (NFPA 1561, 2022; FAA, 2020).

# TACTICS AND STRATEGIES FOR AIRCRAFT FIREFIGHTING

Intervention protocols are indispensable tools for the management of aeronautical emergencies under the Incident Command System. Clearly differentiated from procedures, protocols provide a strategic framework that guides critical decisions during an incident. Effective implementation of these protocols, in conjunction with the flexible and scalable structure of the ICS, ensures that resources are used efficiently, institutions work in a coordinated manner and risks are minimized.

Successful response planning depends on proper training of personnel, integration of multiple institutions, and continuous updating of protocols based on lessons learned. Through a structured and adaptive approach, Aircraft Rescue Firefighters and other key players can respond accurately and effectively to any emergency that arises in the airport environment.

NFPA 424 provides a detailed and effective framework for airport emergency planning, ranging from risk assessment and interagency coordination to the definition of operating procedures and community integration. As leaders in operational safety, it is essential that airport planners adopt these guidelines and adapt them to the specifics of their facilities. Through detailed planning, the execution of drills and collaboration with external institutions, airports can be better prepared to face any type of emergency, ensuring the safety of passengers, staff and airport infrastructure.

The "P" for planning in the Incident Command System is an essential function that ensures the effective organization and execution of emergency response. In the airport context, where the complexity of incidents can vary significantly, detailed and coordinated planning is key to reducing risks, safeguarding lives and minimizing damage to critical infrastructure. Through the proper use of the planning cycle, the institutions involved can be better prepared to face any incident in an efficient and organized manner.

## TACTICS AND STRATEGIES FOR AIRCRAFT FIREFIGHTING

The design of an Incident Action Plan (IAP) is an essential component of airport emergency response. Through the use of SMART objectives, clear strategies and precise tactics, response teams can act quickly and in a coordinated manner to mitigate the effects of the incident. The use of standardized planning tools, such as ICS forms, ensures that all stakeholders are aligned and that flexibility is maintained to adjust the IAP as the needs of the incident change. Effective planning is ultimately the key factor that determines the success of an airport emergency response.

Classification and categorization of resources are fundamental processes in emergency response planning and execution. Standardization and categorization of resources not only facilitates rapid and efficient response, but also ensures interoperability between institutions during large-scale incidents. By following FEMA and USAID BHA guidelines, airports and emergency institutions can significantly improve their response capabilities and ensure that the resources mobilized are appropriate for each type of incident. Proactive planning, based on resource typing, is essential to safeguard lives and protect critical infrastructure during airport emergencies.

Standby levels and command modes are essential tools in the planning and execution of aeronautical emergency response. Proper implementation of these concepts allows response teams to act in a coordinated and effective manner, adjusting their approach based on the severity of the incident and available resources. The flexibility of the Incident commander to switch between command modes, and the ability to mobilize resources at different standby levels, are critical factors for successful operations. By following NFPA, ICAO and FAA regulations, and the best practices described by Brunacini, responders can optimize their performance in critical situations.

The Personnel Counting System is an essential tool for the management of aeronautical emergencies. Its proper implementation enables accurate personnel control, improves operational coordination and ensures the safety of responders. Based on NFPA regulations and emergency management best practices, a well-structured PCS contributes significantly to the success of the operation and minimizes the risks associated with large-scale incidents. The integration of advanced technologies and constant training are key factors to ensure the effectiveness of the PCS in any emergency scenario.

## TACTICS AND STRATEGIES FOR AIRCRAFT FIREFIGHTING

### References

FAA (2020). *Aircraft rescue and firefighting plan (Advisory Circular 150/5210-17C)*. Federal Aviation Administration.

ICAO. (2019). *Airport Services Manual - Part 1: Rescue and Firefighting*. International Civil Aviation Organization.

NFPA. (2022). *NFPA 1561: Standard on Emergency Services Incident Management System and Command Safety*. National Fire Protection Association.

NFPA. (2022). *NFPA 403: Standard for Aircraft Rescue and Fire-Fighting Services at Airports. National Fire Protection Association.*

*NTSB. (2014). Accident Report: Crash of Asiana Airlines Flight 214. National Transportation Safety Board.*

*NFPA. (2018).* NFPA 472: Standard for Competence of Responders to Hazardous Materials Incidents. *National Fire Protection Association.*

*USAID BHA (2021).* Incident Command System Operations Manual. *USAID Bureau for Humanitarian Assistance.*

*IFSTA (2019). Aircraft Rescue and Fire Fighting. International Fire Service Training Association.*

*NFPA. (2022). NFPA 424: Guide for Airport/Community Emergency Planning. National Fire Protection Association.*

FEMA (2010). *National Incident Management System Incident Command System Forms Booklet.*

Incident Command System (ICS) Manual (2014). *ICS field manual.* USAID BHA.

National Incident Management System (NIMS) (2021). *Incident Complexity Guide: Planning, Preparedness and Training.*

# TACTICS AND STRATEGIES FOR AIRCRAFT FIREFIGHTING

Brunacini, A. (2002). *Fire Command.* National Fire Protection Association.

# CHAPTER 3

# IMPLEMENTING THE ACTION PLAN

# TACTICS AND STRATEGIES FOR AIRCRAFT FIREFIGHTING

## INTRODUCTION

The implementation of the Incident Action Plan (IAP) is a crucial stage in the management of aeronautical emergencies, as it puts into practice the strategies and tactics previously planned to address the situation effectively and safely. The AIP is the result of rigorous planning that establishes clear objectives, allocates adequate resources, and defines the specific actions to be taken to control the emergency. In this phase, the ability to execute the plan in an orderly and coordinated manner is critical to mitigating risks and saving lives.

Based on regulations from the *National Fire Protection Association* (NFPA), the *International Civil Aviation Organization (ICAO),* and the *Federal Aviation Administration* (FAA), the implementation of the AIP requires that all responders have a clear understanding of their roles and responsibilities, ensuring a quick and efficient response. According to NFPA 1561, a well-structured command system allows for proper assignment of tasks and ensures that safety is maintained at the incident scene (NFPA, 2022). Through the *Incident Command System* (ICS), emergency leaders have the ability to adapt the plan as the situation evolves, adjusting strategies and allocating additional resources as needed.

In incidents involving aircraft, the complexity of operations requires a flexible and adaptable approach. *ICAO* and the *FAA* state that airports must be prepared to handle a wide variety of emergency scenarios, from aircraft fires to mass evacuations, and EPI implementation must be dynamic enough to adapt to these situations. The *ICAO Airport Rescue and Fire Fighting Manual* stresses the importance of coordination between on-scene responders, ensuring that resources are deployed efficiently and that communications are smooth and effective (ICAO, 2019).

The implementation of the IAP also includes constant monitoring and adjustment of the plan in real time. According to the recommendations of the *ICAO CRESIA Course* on Airport Safety, it is critical that incident commanders maintain a holistic view of the operation, continuously monitoring conditions and making informed decisions to adapt the IAP to changing circumstances (ICAO, 2021). In addition, the *International Fire Service Training Association* (IFSTA) emphasizes that effective execution of the IAP relies heavily on the ongoing training and coaching of response personnel. Regular drills allow aeronautical fire crews and other responders to be familiar with the procedures and be able to react quickly and accurately during a real emergency (IFSTA, 2018).

In this chapter, we will explore the challenges and best practices in the implementation of the AIP, considering examples of success in actual aviation emergencies and how lessons learned have improved the effectiveness of future responses. The ability of responders to execute the IAP in a disciplined and adaptive manner is a determining factor in reducing damage and protecting life at aeronautical incidents.

In this chapter we will explore 2 essential points that must remain in your DNA, exterior and interior securing, we will address tactical priorities, the response sequence and we will delve into each of the possible scenarios that could arise in the response to emergencies with aircraft.

## TACTICS AND STRATEGIES FOR AIRCRAFT FIREFIGHTING

### 3.1 Tactical Priorities

The implementation of the Incident Action Plan (IAP) in aviation emergencies is guided by three fundamental tactical priorities: protect life, stabilize the incident, and preserve property and the environment. These priorities, based on international standards such as the *National Fire Protection Association* (NFPA), the *International Civil Aviation Organization (ICAO),* and the *Federal Aviation Administration* (FAA), provide a

framework to guide the actions of responders. The ability to execute these priorities effectively is key to reducing risk, mitigating the impact of the incident, and ensuring the safety of everyone involved.

The structure of these tactical priorities not only facilitates immediate response, but also ensures that aeronautical fire crews and other emergency services act in a coordinated manner aligned with the objectives of the EPI. In addition, proper implementation of these priorities requires constant assessment of the operational scenario, flexibility to adapt to changing incident conditions, and seamless communication between the different teams involved (NFPA 1561, 2022; ICAO, 2019).

### 3.1.1 Protecting Life

The protection of human life is the top tactical priority in any aviation emergency. This includes not only the lives of the passengers and crew of the affected aircraft, but also the lives of the response personnel involved in the incident. According to NFPA 403 (2022), aeronautical fire personnel must be able to execute rescue and firefighting operations with speed and precision, focusing on the safe evacuation of people trapped in the aircraft or exposed to imminent hazards such as fire, explosion or structural collapse.

The concept of "protecting life" extends to the creation of safe evacuation routes, the immediate stabilization of victims through primary medical care and the protection of responders with appropriate protective equipment. The *ICAO Airport Services Manual* (2019) standard states that responders must be prepared to intervene in various types of emergencies, from fires to collision situations, and must follow clearly defined protocols to ensure orderly evacuation and prompt care for the injured.

In practice, the priority of protecting life includes the following specific actions:

- **Rapid Evacuation**: Implement procedures for the rapid and safe evacuation of aircraft occupants, using unobstructed access routes and coordinating with other services such as medical teams.
- **Search and rescue**: Use specialized equipment, such as thermal cameras, to locate victims who may be trapped inside the aircraft or in areas that are difficult to access.
- **Immediate medical care**: Provide primary medical care at the scene of the incident and coordinate the transfer of victims to medical facilities if necessary.

The ultimate goal of this priority is to minimize the loss of human life and ensure that all those affected receive adequate care in the shortest possible time.

### 3.1.2 Incident Stabilization

Incident stabilization is the second tactical priority and refers to controlling the emergency situation to prevent it from worsening. Once human life has been protected, aeronautical fire crews must focus on containing the hazards present, such as fire, fuel spills, or the threat of explosions, which can result from the unique characteristics of aircraft and airport infrastructure.

*According to NFPA 1561* (2022) and *FAA* regulations (2020), incident stabilization includes actions such as:

- **Fire Extinguishing**: Apply appropriate techniques and agents to effectively extinguish the fire. This may include the use of aqueous film forming foam (AFFF),  water, or chemicals depending on the type of fire and materials present.

- **Spill control**: In situations where there are spills of fuel or other hazardous materials, equipment must contain and neutralize these products to avoid secondary fires or environmental contamination. The use of containment booms and absorbent products is key in these operations.

- **Ensure structural stability**: If the aircraft has suffered significant structural damage, teams must work to secure the unstable parts, avoiding additional collapses that put rescuers and victims at risk.

Stabilization is a dynamic process that requires constant assessment of incident conditions. Incident commanders, following the *Incident Command System* (ICS) principles established by USAID BHA (2021), must adapt their tactics as the situation develops, ensuring that resources are allocated efficiently and operations are safe and coordinated.

## TACTICS AND STRATEGIES FOR AIRCRAFT FIREFIGHTING

### 3.1.3 Property and Environmental Conservation

Preservation of property and the environment is the third tactical priority in the implementation of the IAP. Once life has been secured and the incident has been stabilized, measures need to be taken to minimize property damage and reduce environmental impact. In the context of aeronautical emergencies, this involves protecting both the aircraft and the airport infrastructure, and preventing collateral damage that may result from the incident.

*NFPA 403* and *ICAO* (2019) stress the importance of acting in a manner that prevents major damage to critical facilities, such as fuel depots, hangars, and runways. In addition, it is critical that responders follow strict protocols to avoid environmental contamination, particularly in cases where there are spills of fuel or hazardous substances. This includes the use of absorbent materials, proper containment of spills, and remediation of affected soil or water.

**Specific actions under this tactical priority include:**

- **Protection of airport infrastructure**: Coordinate efforts to protect critical facilities such as fuel depots, service areas and nearby hangars, minimizing the risk of secondary fires.
- **Environmental control**: Use containment and neutralization techniques for hazardous substances to prevent chemicals from reaching water bodies or sensitive areas.
- **Damage assessment**: Once the incident has been stabilized, conduct a damage assessment to identify areas that require immediate repair and those that can be addressed in the long term.

Property conservation and environmental protection are key responsibilities for aeronautical fire crews, not only to minimize incident costs, but also to comply with international safety and sustainability regulations.

## 3.2 Response Sequence

The response sequence in an aeronautical emergency is a highly structured process that follows a series of phases designed to ensure a safe, rapid and effective intervention. Proper execution of the response sequence is essential to minimize the impact of the incident, protect human life, stabilize the scene and preserve both property and the environment. Based on *National Fire Protection Association* (NFPA), *International Civil Aviation Organization (ICAO),* and *Federal Aviation Administration* (FAA) regulations, the response sequence includes key phases such as incident assessment, situation reporting using the LCANS format, spontaneous evacuation assistance, and airframe protection (NFPA 1561, 2022; ICAO, 2019).

### 3.2.1 Evaluation

The initial incident assessment is the first step in any response sequence. In this phase, the Incident commander and aeronautical fire crews conduct a reconnaissance of the situation, identifying immediate hazards, the number of people involved, and environmental conditions, such as the presence of fire or fuel spills. The assessment is crucial to establish a clear picture of the incident, which will allow informed decisions to be made and resources to be deployed effectively (USAID BHA, 2021).

During this phase, factors such as the exact location of the aircraft, the nature of the damage, the number of passengers and crew, and the possibility of hazardous materials in the area must be considered. *NFPA 403* states that the assessment should be performed quickly but accurately, as the effectiveness of the following phases of the Incident Action Plan will depend on it (NFPA, 2022).

### 3.2.1.1 LCANS Report

The **LCANS** (Location, Condition, Actions, Needs and Safety) report is a critical communication tool during the initial assessment. This standardized report allows  aeronautical fire crews to convey clear and concise situation information to the Incident commander and other stakeholders. *NFPA 1561* stresses the importance of standardization in situation reports to ensure that all information is understandable and that teams can act based on accurate data (NFPA, 2022).

1. **Location**: Indicates the exact location of the aircraft and the affected areas.
2. **Condition**: Describes the condition of the incident, such as the size of the fire, the number of passengers involved or the presence of hazardous materials.
3. **Actions**: Lists immediate actions being taken, such as extinguishing the fire or evacuating passengers.
4. **Needs**: Sets forth additional needs, such as resources, equipment, or specialized personnel.
5. **Safety**: Identifies any additional hazards, such as the possibility of explosions or the need for exclusion zones to protect emergency personnel.

The **LCANS** report not only facilitates coordination between teams on the ground, but also allows the Incident commander to adjust the IAP according to changing incident conditions. This type of effective communication is critical to successful emergency management (ICAO, 2019).

### 3.2.1.2 Spontaneous Evacuation Assistance

During an aircraft emergency, it is common for passengers and crew to attempt to evacuate the aircraft spontaneously, before emergency crews arrive on the scene. Assisting in this spontaneous evacuation is a tactical priority  during the initial phases of the incident. Aeronautical fire crews should be prepared to facilitate this evacuation, directing people to safe areas and providing medical assistance if necessary.

ICAO regulations and the FAA operations manual state that evacuation should be conducted in an orderly manner, minimizing the risk of panic or further injury. Aircraft Rescue Firefighters should coordinate with aircraft personnel to ensure that all emergency exits are operational and clear of obstructions and should be equipped with appropriate equipment to assist in the evacuation, such as rapid evacuation stretchers and respiratory protective equipment in case of fire (FAA, 2020).

The main challenge in this phase is to ensure that spontaneous evacuation does not interfere with firefighting operations or other critical actions. Fire crews must create safety perimeters and ensure that evacuees are moved to safe areas away from potential explosions or fuel spills (NFPA 403, 2022).

### 3.2.1.3 Fuselage Protection (External Securing)

Once evacuation is underway, it is crucial to protect the aircraft fuselage to prevent the fire from spreading and causing additional damage. Airframe protection, also known as external securing, involves the use of firefighting vehicles and other specialized equipment to apply extinguishing agents, such as AFFF foam, to key areas of the aircraft.

According *to NFPA 403*, airframe protection is a tactical priority that must be conducted simultaneously with other actions, such as evacuation and spill control. Proper application of foam and water can prevent the fire from spreading to the interior of the aircraft or to nearby areas, such as fuel tanks. This phase also includes continuous monitoring of the airframe temperature, using heat detection equipment to ensure that secondary fires do not occur (NFPA 1561, 2022).

In addition, airframe protection is critical to ensure that rescue teams can safely enter the aircraft to conduct search and rescue operations. Incident commanders must effectively coordinate between teams conducting fire suppression and teams tasked with evacuation and rescue, ensuring that the two work in harmony to avoid interference (USAID BHA, 2021).

### 3.2.2 Fire Control (Q1)

Fire control is one of the most critical phases of aeronautical emergency response. At this stage, aeronautical firefighting teams must be able to control fires quickly and accurately, using the appropriate techniques and equipment, while protecting occupants, aircraft egress media such as emergency sliders, as well as airport infrastructure. The key to success in aircraft fire control lies in the speed with which it acts, the command mode that is normally selected in this phase the officer in charge orders rapid attack mode with

"Bombing", is a blitz attack, the correct selection of extinguishing agents (only foam? Or dual attack (foam and PQS?), and the coordination between the different teams involved. This control is carried out in accordance with international regulations such as those of the *National Fire Protection Association* (NFPA), the *International Civil Aviation Organization (ICAO),* and the *Federal Aviation Administration* (FAA), which provide a regulatory framework to ensure safety during this type of interventions (NFPA 403, 2022; ICAO, 2019).

## Evaluation of the Situation and Choice of Extinguishing Agents

The first step in fire control is the accurate assessment of the type of fire (two-dimensional or three-dimensional), its location and the risk it poses to the airframe. According to *NFPA 403*, it is essential that aeronautical firefighting teams perform a rapid

assessment of the scenario to determine which type of extinguishing agent will be most effective (NFPA, 2022).

The use of aqueous film-forming foam (AFFF) and PQS dry chemical powders would be the most recommended in fuel fires, as it covers the surface and suffocates the fire by preventing oxygen from contacting the fuel. NFPA and *ICAO* also suggest the use of gaseous extinguishing agents, such as carbon dioxide ($CO_2$), on electrical fires or in areas where water or foam would not be effective (ICAO, 2019).

It is essential that teams select the correct agent to prevent the spread of the agent and protect both people and the aircraft structure.

### Fire Control Application: Stage Q1

In the context of aeronautical firefighting, the term "Q1" refers to the initial stage in which fire control is implemented through the use of high-capacity extinguishing agents. During this stage, ARFF (Aircraft Rescue and Fire Fighting) vehicles are deployed at strategic points to attack the fire from different angles and reduce the intensity of the fire. The main objective of the Q1 stage is to prevent the fire from spreading inside the aircraft and to mitigate the risk of explosions resulting from fuel ignition (FAA, 2020).

According to *NFPA 403*, firefighters should employ either direct or indirect attack techniques, depending on the access  to the fire. Direct attack is performed when the fire is visible and accessible, while indirect attack is used when the fire is confined to areas such as cargo compartments or fuel tanks. In the Q1 phase, it is key that the teams work in coordination, applying the right amount of foam or water to extinguish the fire without compromising the integrity of the aircraft.

## Coordination and Communication during Fire Control

Coordination is a determining factor for the success of fire control in aeronautical emergencies. The *Incident Command System* (ICS) states that the Incident Commander must have a complete view of the operation, ensuring that response teams, from firefighters to technical support personnel, work under a clear and effective command structure (USAID BHA, 2021). This seamless communication is crucial to avoid duplication of effort and ensure that the fire is attacked from different points without putting firefighters at risk.

In addition, personnel protection is a priority. Crews must wear appropriate personal protective equipment and follow strict safety protocols to avoid injury from explosions or exposure to hazardous materials. According to *NFPA 1500*, aeronautical firefighting crews must be trained to perform under pressure, applying extinguishing techniques while remaining aware of the risks of structural collapse or secondary fires (NFPA, 2022).

## Successful Fire Control Examples

An emblematic example of a successful fire control operation occurred during the crash of Air France Flight 358 at Toronto airport in 2005. In this case, the fire originated after a crash landing caused the aircraft to catch fire as it left the runway. Thanks to the rapid intervention of Aircraft Rescue Firefighters, who applied AFFF foam from multiple ARFF vehicles, the fire was brought under control and all passengers were evacuated without fatalities (TSB, 2005).

## TACTICS AND STRATEGIES FOR AIRCRAFT FIREFIGHTING

These types of successful interventions underline the importance of the Q1 phase in firefighting and the need for pre-planning, constant training and efficient coordination between response teams.

### 3.2.3 Rescue (Primary Search)

The rescue of victims during an aeronautical emergency is one of the most critical phases within the response sequence. Within this category, the primary search refers to the first rapid and systematic inspection of the aircraft and affected areas, with the objective of locating and evacuating victims who may be trapped or unable to leave by their own means. This process must be carried out efficiently and safely, maximizing the chances of saving lives while minimizing risks to rescuers.

Primary search in aeronautical emergencies follows the guidelines of international regulations such as the *National Fire Protection Association* (NFPA), the *International Civil Aviation Organization (ICAO),* and the *Federal Aviation Administration* (FAA), which establish standardized procedures for the management of these operations. These regulations are designed to ensure that rescue is conducted in an organized, coordinated, and safe manner (NFPA 403, 2022; ICAO, 2019).

### Rapid Assessment and Incident Command System

The first step in the primary search is the initial assessment of the incident. The incident commander, under the *Incident Command System* (ICS), should assign search and rescue teams to critical areas of the aircraft based on preliminary analysis of damage and the status of fire or other hazards. *NFPA 1561* stresses the importance of rapid and accurate assessment to guide rescue operations in a safe and effective manner (NFPA, 2022). In situations where access to the aircraft is limited due to fire or structural collapse, it is critical that teams consistently assess hazards before entering the airframe.

The use of thermal imagers and other detection equipment is critical during primary search, as it allows rescuers to locate victims in low visibility conditions, such as dense smoke or low-light areas. Search technology is especially useful on large aircraft, where the number of compartments can make it difficult to locate passengers without advanced detection tools (IFSTA, 2018).

## Search and Rescue Procedures

The primary search is based on speed and systematicity, dividing the aircraft into priority sectors or zones. According to *NFPA 403* recommendations, Aircraft Rescue Firefighters should conduct the search in organized teams, starting with the highest risk areas, such as passenger compartments and the cabin, where victims are most likely to be found. This tactic ensures that the most critical areas are covered immediately, which maximizes the likelihood of finding and rescuing victims quickly (NFPA, 2022).

Key phases of primary rescue include:

1. **Safe access to the aircraft**: Rescue teams must access the aircraft safely, using controlled entry routes and ensuring that emergency exits are operational. In many cases, it is necessary to use specialized tools, such as fuselage cutters, to open blocked or damaged areas.
2. **Review of critical areas**: The review begins in locations where victims are suspected to be trapped, such as passenger seats, the flight deck, and crew service areas. During this phase, rescuers must work systematically, checking each compartment and making sure that no victims remain unaccounted for.
3. **Constant Communication**: Primary search teams should maintain constant communication with the Incident commander to report progress and any significant findings. Smooth communication is key to coordinating operations and ensuring that any changes in incident conditions, such as fire spread or structural collapse, are immediately

communicated to teams on the ground (USAID BHA, 2021).

### Victim Assistance and Evacuation

Once victims are located during the primary search, rescue teams must provide immediate assistance and assess the physical condition of the survivors. In many cases, victims may be unconscious or seriously injured, requiring rapid evacuation

procedures using stretchers and other life support equipment. According *to NFPA 402* (2022), rescuers must be prepared to administer first aid and stabilize the victims before moving them to safe areas where medical teams in the CVA victim concentration area can intervene, it is necessary to clarify that inside the aircraft we only verify if the person has signs of life or not, After this action, in an intermediate zone, our pre-hospital care team must be trained to attend the injured, stabilize them and classify them using a more structured Triage method. In Colombia, 5 colors are used (Penta polar), while in other countries only 4 colors are used (tetrapolar).

Safe evacuation also involves ensuring that exit routes are clear and protected against any hazards, such as fire spread or falling debris. Rescuers should ensure that victims are moved out of the danger area as quickly as possible and should work in coordination with the LCA medical teams so that patients are treated quickly and efficiently (ICAO, 2019).

# TACTICS AND STRATEGIES FOR AIRCRAFT FIREFIGHTING

## Primary Search Success Stories

A successful example of primary search in an aviation emergency is the 2013 crash of Asiana Airlines Flight 214 at San Francisco International Airport. Despite difficult conditions due to a fire that originated in the rear of the aircraft, rescue teams managed to locate and evacuate most of the passengers within the first few minutes, using rapid search techniques and effective communication with the Incident commander. The rapid intervention and application of primary search protocols saved the lives of dozens of people (NTSB, 2014).

These types of examples highlight the importance of preparation and accurate execution of the primary search in aircraft incidents. The ability of aeronautical fire crews to locate and evacuate victims quickly is key to reducing fatalities in emergencies of this nature.

## Challenges and Best Practices

One of the biggest challenges in primary search is the constant risk to rescue teams, especially in conditions where fire, fuel spills or structural damage compromise airframe safety. It is essential that Aircraft Rescue Firefighters are properly trained and equipped to operate in these conditions, strictly following safety protocols established by NFPA and other international organizations (NFPA 1561, 2022).

Best practices include conducting regular drills and using advanced technology to enhance search and rescue capabilities. The integration of thermal cameras, drones and motion sensors can significantly increase search efficiency, especially in areas of difficult access or low visibility. In addition, ongoing training in the use of personal protective equipment (PPE) and search procedures ensures that rescue teams are prepared to deal with any emergency situation involving aircraft.

## TACTICS AND STRATEGIES FOR AIRCRAFT FIREFIGHTING

### 3.2.4 Fire Suppression (Exterior Securing and Interior Securing) (Q2 and Q3)

Fire suppression in an aeronautical emergency is a critical phase within the Incident Action Plan (IAP), in which specific techniques and tactics must be employed for both exterior securing (Q2) and interior securing (Q3). The main objective of these phases is to contain and extinguish the fire, ensuring the safety of occupants and response personnel. These operations are carried out in strict compliance with the regulations established by the *National Fire Protection Association* (NFPA), the *International Civil Aviation Organization (ICAO),* and the *Federal Aviation Administration* (FAA). In addition, the *Incident Command System* (ICS) and USAID BHA protocols provide a framework that ensures these operations are conducted in an organized and efficient manner (NFPA 403, 2022; ICAO, 2019).

**Phase Q2: External Assurance**

**Exterior securing (Q2)** refers to the initial actions Aircraft Rescue Firefighters take to control and extinguish the fire on the exterior of the aircraft. This phase is activated  immediately after the initial assessment of the incident and the implementation of the first resources. The priority in Q2 is to prevent the spread of the fire to other areas of the aircraft or to critical airport infrastructure such as fuel tanks, hangars or runways.

According to *NFPA 403* regulations, crews must deploy ARFF (Aircraft Rescue and Fire Fighting) vehicles at strategic points around the aircraft to attack the fire from different angles. The use of AFFF (Aqueous Film Forming Foam) foam is key in this phase, as it creates a barrier between the fire and oxygen, which helps to smother the flames and prevent the fire from rekindling (NFPA 403, 2022).

Proper application of extinguishing agents and coordination between firefighting teams are essential to ensure the effectiveness of exterior securing. Incident commanders should allocate resources according to fire conditions, prioritizing critical areas such as aircraft engines, planes (where fuel is stored) and landing gear. In situations where there is a significant risk of explosion due to fuel spills, containment barriers should be implemented to prevent the spread of fire (ICAO, 2019).

A fundamental aspect of exterior securing is the protection of rescuers and people who may still be near the aircraft. Fire control from the outside must be carried out in a safe manner, ensuring that evacuation routes are clear and that the fire does not spread to areas where victims or rescue teams are located. Coordination between extinguishing actions and rescue operations is key to minimize risks (FAA, 2020).

## Phase Q3: Interior Assurance

**Interior securing (Q3)** refers to fire suppression actions inside the aircraft, once the exterior securing has been partially successful or is under control. This phase is of utmost importance to prevent the fire from spreading to passenger compartments or critical areas within the aircraft structure, such as electrical systems, internal fuel tanks or cargo compartments.

*NFPA 403* states that Aircraft Rescue Firefighters must be equipped with respiratory protective equipment and specialized tools to safely access the interior of the aircraft. The use of thermal cameras is critical in this phase, as it allows rescuers to detect hot spots that are not visible to the naked eye, helping them to locate pockets of fire that are still active or could rekindle (NFPA 1561, 2022).

## TACTICS AND STRATEGIES FOR AIRCRAFT FIREFIGHTING

In phase Q3, firefighting teams must apply a combination of direct and indirect attack techniques. Direct attack is performed when firefighters have visual access to the fire and can apply foam or water directly to the flames. Indirect attack, on the other hand, is necessary in situations where the fire is confined to areas that are difficult to access, such as cargo compartments. In these cases, penetrating devices are used to inject foam or extinguishing gases into the confined spaces (IFSTA, 2018).

Phase Q3 also involves constant assessment of the structural integrity of the aircraft. It is essential that firefighters monitor heat levels and any signs of potential collapse while conducting operations inside the aircraft. According to *NFPA 1500* (2022), equipment should be removed immediately if fire conditions or the aircraft structure suddenly changes, putting its safety at risk.

### Coordination between External and Internal Assurance

One of the keys to successful fire suppression in an aeronautical emergency is coordination between the exterior and interior securing phases. Incident commanders must ensure that both phases occur simultaneously, but do not interfere with each other. Proper sequencing of these actions ensures that the fire is controlled both outside and inside the aircraft, minimizing the risk of the fire spreading or rekindling (USAID BHA, 2021).

In many situations, exterior securing provides a window of
opportunity for rescue
teams to safely enter the
aircraft and perform interior
securing. Firefighters must
coordinate their efforts so
that resources are deployed
efficiently, ensuring that
critical points of the fire are
covered quickly. In some
cases, specialized
extinguishing vehicles that
can operate both outside
and inside the aircraft may be required, depending on the type of fire
and aircraft structure (FAA, 2020).

## Fire Suppression Success Example

An emblematic example of the correct implementation of phases Q2
and Q3 can be found in the 1989 crash of United Airlines Flight 232.
In this incident, the aircraft suffered a crash landing that resulted in
a massive fire. Aeronautical fire crews were able to contain the fire
by exterior securing, which allowed rescue crews to safely enter the
aircraft and extinguish the internal fires. Despite the severity of the
accident, the rapid response and effective suppression of the fire
minimized the loss of life and prevented a major catastrophe (NTSB,
1990).

## 3.2.5 Removal and Revision (Secondary Search)

Once the fire has been controlled and the initial situation has been
stabilized, the removal and overhaul phase, also known as secondary
search, begins. It is important to emphasize that the team conducting
the secondary search must be different from the one conducting the
primary search to avoid bias. This phase is critical to ensure that there
are no active pockets of fire, to rescue any possible victims not
located in the primary search, and to thoroughly review all areas

affected by the incident. The removal and overhaul process is conducted in accordance with international regulations established by the *National Fire Protection Association* (NFPA), the *International Civil Aviation Organization (ICAO)*, the *Federal Aviation Administration* (FAA) and following the principles of the *Incident Command System* (ICS) as recommended by USAID BHA (NFPA 1561, 2022; ICAO, 2019).

**Importance of Secondary Search**

The secondary search, or overhaul, is a critical stage in ensuring that the incident is fully under control. During the primary search, efforts are focused on locating and evacuating victims in easily accessible areas, while the secondary search involves a much more detailed inspection of all compartments and structures of the aircraft, including hard-to-reach areas such as cargo compartments, the cockpit, or small spaces in which victims may have become trapped. According to *NFPA 403*, secondary search is essential to ensure that there are no unevacuated victims or latent fire sources (NFPA, 2022).

The secondary search also aims to ensure that the fire is completely extinguished. This includes removing embers, checking spaces where incandescent materials might be present, and removing debris that could conceal potential hot spots. The use of thermal cameras and heat detection equipment is essential during this phase to identify any signs of residual heat in the aircraft or surrounding areas. This is especially important in situations where fires have been controlled, but re-ignition risks still exist (IFSTA, 2018).

**Removal and Review Procedures**

Removal and overhaul procedures involve a series of steps designed to ensure that the affected area is safe and free of hazards. *NFPA 1500* (2022) states that aeronautical fire crews must follow a strict protocol that includes the systematic review of all areas where fire may have spread or where structural damage could have trapped victims. This review must be meticulous and exhaustive, ensuring that no compartment or critical area of the aircraft is omitted.

1. **Structure Review**: During the secondary search, teams should carefully review the aircraft structure, looking for signs of weakness or collapse that could put rescuers or responders at risk. According to the *FAA* (2020), it is critical to assess any damage to the planes, fuselage, and landing gear structure, areas that may have been compromised by the extreme heat or impact of the crash landing.

2. **Hot spot detection**: The use of thermal cameras is crucial to detect hot spots that are not visible to the naked eye. These hot spots could be hidden under debris or in confined areas of the aircraft. Early detection of these spots can prevent secondary fires, which is particularly important in incidents where large amounts of fuel are involved (ICAO, 2019).

3. **Debris removal**: Debris removal is a critical part of the search. In many cases, collapsed structures or damaged compartments may have trapped victims that were not located during the primary search. Fire crews must carefully remove debris to ensure that there are no trapped persons or hidden fire sources.

4. **Electrical and fuel systems check**: In the overhaul phase, the aircraft's electrical and fuel systems should also be inspected, as these may represent a potential source of re-ignition. *NFPA 403* regulations recommend checking the aircraft's electrical systems for short circuits or areas where heat may have damaged wiring. Similarly, fuel tanks should be checked to ensure that there are no leaks that could cause an explosion or secondary fire (NFPA, 2022).

**Secondary Search Coordination and Communication**

Coordination and communication between response teams are vital during a secondary search. The *Incident Command System* (ICS) provides an organizational framework that facilitates the assignment of teams to different areas of the aircraft and ensures that all actions are performed safely and efficiently (USAID BHA, 2021). Incident commanders must ensure that teams maintain constant communication and that any findings are reported immediately to enable quick and accurate decision making.

During the removal and examination, it is essential that teams work in conjunction with medical services and other support teams. If victims are found during this phase, they should be evacuated immediately and receive medical attention. The priority in the secondary search is to ensure that no victims remain unrescued and that the area is completely safe for further investigation and restoration (ICAO, 2019).

### Example of Success in Secondary Research

An example of the correct implementation of the secondary search occurred during the crash of British Airways Flight 268 in 2008, where the aircraft made an emergency landing at Heathrow Airport. After the initial evacuation and control of the fire, fire crews conducted a thorough secondary search, which allowed the location of hidden hot spots in the cargo cabin that had not been detected during the primary search. This intervention prevented the fire from rekindling and ensured the safety of the investigation team that entered later to assess the damage (NTSB, 2008).

### Challenges and Best Practices

Secondary search presents a number of challenges, particularly in incidents where fire has caused severe structural damage or where the aircraft's electrical and fuel systems pose an ongoing hazard. The key to overcoming these challenges is constant preparation and training of personnel. *NFPA 1500* regulations suggest that fire crews regularly participate in drills that include complex removal and overhaul scenarios, ensuring that they are prepared to deal with any situation that may arise during the secondary search (NFPA, 2022).

Another recommended practice is the use of advanced technology, such as drones equipped with thermal cameras, to facilitate the review of difficult-to-access areas. These technologies allow rescue teams to make more accurate and detailed assessments without putting firefighters at risk.

### 3.3 External Underwriting

Exterior securing in an aircraft emergency is a fundamental aspect of the fire and spill response strategy. This process involves the containment of hazards found on the exterior of the aircraft, such as fuel spills, fires in specific areas such as engines, landing gear, and cargo compartments. Regulations from the *National Fire Protection Association* (NFPA), the *International Civil Aviation Organization (ICAO),* and the *Federal Aviation Administration* (FAA) establish clear and detailed procedures to manage these hazards effectively and safely, ensuring that rescue and fire control operations can proceed smoothly (NFPA 403, 2022; ICAO, 2019).

### 3.3.1 Non-Fire Fuel Spills (Small, Medium, Large)

One of the most common risks in aeronautical emergencies is fuel spillage. This type of incident can occur during a forced landing, a collision, or a rupture in the fuel supply system. The management of these spills is divided into three categories according to their size: small, medium, and large, and each requires different tactics.

- **Small Spills**: These usually cover a limited area, generally less than 1 square meter. According to *NFPA 403*, firefighting teams must contain these spills with absorbent materials, this action is called confinement, preventing the fuel from coming into contact with ignition sources. The use of extinguishing foams can also be effective in preventing the evaporation of flammable liquids (NFPA, 2022).

- **Medium Spills**: Medium-sized spills (up to 10 square meters) require more rapid and effective containment. Firefighters should deploy containment booms and use AFFF foam to reduce the risk of ignition. In addition, they should ensure that ventilation in the area is adequate to prevent the accumulation of fuel vapors (ICAO, 2019).
- **Large Spills**: In large spills, which can cover areas greater than 10 square meters, the response must be immediate and massive. According to the *FAA* and *NFPA*, teams should deploy multiple lines of AFFF foam to completely cover the spill, preventing a potential ignition. Evacuation of the affected area is critical in these cases to minimize the risk of explosion (FAA, 2020).

### 3.3.2 Two- and three-dimensional fires

Controlling two- and three-dimensional fires presents a particular challenge for aeronautical firefighting crews. Two-dimensional fires spread on flat surfaces, such as the runway or aircraft fuselage, while three-dimensional fires involve fuels burning on multiple planes, such as in pipes or running engines.

- **Two-Dimensional Fires**: These fires, often caused by igniting fuel spills, require extensive use of AFFF foam to cover the burning surface. *NFPA 403* recommends the use of ARFF vehicles that can project foam from a safe distance to prevent the fire from spreading (NFPA, 2022).

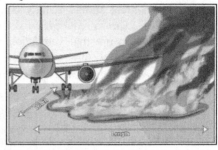

- **Three-Dimensional Fires**: Three-dimensional fires, which may involve fuels dripping or flowing from vertical or sloping surfaces, are more difficult to control. According to the *FAA*, firefighters must use direct attack techniques with gaseous or powdered extinguishing agents to cut off the oxygen supply to the fire.

Coordination between teams is essential to ensure that all planes of spread are addressed (FAA, 2020).

## TACTICS AND STRATEGIES FOR AIRCRAFT FIREFIGHTING

### 3.3.3 Cargo Compartment Fires

Cargo compartments, especially on commercial aircraft, present a significant risk during a fire due to the possible presence of hazardous materials or flammable cargo. *ICAO*  and *NFPA* recommend that fire crews use thermal detectors to locate fire within these compartments, as many of them are completely enclosed (ICAO, 2019). In most cases, gas fire suppression systems should be used to extinguish the fire without damaging the airframe or jeopardizing the structural integrity of the aircraft (NFPA, 2022).

### 3.3.4 APU Fires

The **Auxiliary Power Unit** (APU) is a potential source of fire due to heat buildup and the presence of electrical and combustible components in small areas. A fire in the APU can spread rapidly if not controlled immediately. *NFPA 403* regulations recommend the use of specific extinguishing agents for electrical fires, such as carbon dioxide or dry chemical powder, to extinguish these fires without causing major damage to the aircraft electrical systems (NFPA, 2022).

### 3.3.5 Engine Fires

Engine fires represent one of the most dangerous situations for Aircraft Rescue Firefighters, as engines contain large quantities of fuel, lubricating oils and flammable materials. Aircraft engine fires must be tackled using specialized extinguishing agents that do not damage engine components or interfere with flight control.

According to the *FAA* and *ICAO*, firefighters should apply AFFF foam or CO2 directly on the affected engines, making sure to shut off the fuel supply as soon as possible. In addition, it is important to maintain continuous surveillance after initial extinguishment to prevent materials in the engines from overheating and restarting the fire (FAA, 2020; ICAO, 2019).

### 3.3.6 Landing Gear Fires

Emergencies involving aircraft landing gear present a significant challenge to aeronautical fire crews due to the materials involved and the high temperatures that can develop during landing and braking maneuvers. These incidents require detailed technical knowledge of landing gear construction, the risks associated with wheel overheating, and proper extinguishing procedures. Key aspects of these emergencies are explored below, including the management of overheating, the use of extinguishing agents, and the characteristics of the combustible metals involved in landing gear.

## Landing Gear Overheating

During landings, especially on short runways or under maximum load conditions, landing gear brakes can overheat due to the effort required to stop an aircraft at high speed. This phenomenon is known as landing gear overheating, and can have serious consequences if not handled properly. In many cases, the heat generated by the brakes can transfer to the rubber tires, causing them to catch fire if not properly cooled.

Landing gears are designed to withstand high temperatures, but when temperatures exceed certain limits, they can cause component melting. One example is the **fusible plug**, which is designed to melt and release tire pressure when the temperature reaches approximately 177°C (350°F) (IFSTA, 2020). This safety mechanism prevents the tire's internal pressure from rising to dangerous levels that could cause an explosion. However, if overheating persists, landing gear components, including brakes and tires, can be severely affected.

## Use of Nitrogen in Tire Inflation

In modern aircraft, landing gear tires are inflated with nitrogen instead of compressed air. Nitrogen is preferred because it is an inert gas, which means it does not react explosively with heat, unlike the oxygen present in compressed air. This is crucial to avoid fires or explosions in situations where the landing gear overheats. The use of nitrogen also helps maintain a constant pressure inside the tires, even under extreme temperature conditions.

When an overheated tire reaches a critical temperature, the wheels can catch fire. Aircraft tire rubber begins to burn at temperatures above 500°F (260°C) (IFSTA, 2020), and if not properly cooled, can cause fires that are difficult to control. In these situations, it is crucial that responders act immediately to apply the appropriate extinguishing agents and prevent the spread of fire to other critical areas of the aircraft.

### Metals Used in Landing Gear and Ignition Characteristics

Landing gears are manufactured from a variety of metals designed to withstand the extreme loads during landing. The most common metals used in landing gear construction include **aluminum**, **titanium** and **magnesium alloys**. Each of these metals has different ignition characteristics that affect how they behave in a fire and what type of extinguishing agents are needed to suppress it.

- **Aluminum**: This metal is lightweight and corrosion resistant, so it is widely used in the aircraft industry. Although aluminum is not highly flammable, it can melt at temperatures of approximately 660°C (1220°F) and contribute to the spread of a fire if it melts.
- **Titanium**: Used for its high strength and low density, titanium has a higher melting point, around 1668°C (3034°F). However, when titanium comes in contact with oxygen at high temperatures, it can burn with great intensity. Titanium fires require specialized extinguishing agents to prevent the fire from spreading (NFPA, 2022).
- **Magnesium**: Magnesium is particularly dangerous in aircraft fires, as it is

a highly flammable metal. The ignition temperature of magnesium is approximately 473°C (883°F). Once magnesium starts to burn, it can reach extremely high temperatures and is difficult to extinguish with water or AFFF foam, as it reacts violently with these agents, releasing hydrogen, which can aggravate the fire (IFSTA, 2020).

## Fire Extinguishing Agents for Combustible Metals Fires

In fires involving combustible metals, such as magnesium or titanium, conventional extinguishing agents are not effective. Combustible metal fires require the use of **Class D extinguishing powders**, which are specifically designed to suppress these types of fires by smothering flames and absorbing heat. Class D powders, such as graphite powder or sodium chloride, create a barrier that prevents oxygen from feeding the fire, which is crucial for controlling metal fires such as magnesium.

In situations where landing gear contains magnesium or other combustible metal components, the use of these extinguishing agents is essential. According to NFPA regulations and IFSTA recommendations, Aircraft Rescue Firefighters must be equipped with Class D extinguishing powder to deal with these types of fires safely and effectively (IFSTA, 2020).

## 3.4 Interior Assurance

Interior securing in aeronautical emergencies is a critical phase within the Incident Action Plan (IAP) that focuses on fire mitigation and suppression and the execution of search and rescue operations inside the aircraft. This phase involves cutting, suppressing fires, ventilating, and performing primary and secondary searches in the different compartments of the aircraft. Following *National Fire Protection Association* (NFPA), *International Civil Aviation Organization (ICAO),* and *Federal Aviation Administration* (FAA) regulations, interior securing requires meticulous planning, specialized equipment, and effective coordination between rescue and extinguishing teams (NFPA 403, 2022; ICAO, 2019).

### 3.4.1 De-energization and fire suppression procedures from the cockpit

Aircraft Rescue Firefighters should be thoroughly familiar with the cut-off and suppression procedures from the cockpit of an aircraft during emergencies. These procedures include reducing engine power, using engine and APU (Auxiliary Power Unit) fire suppression systems, and disconnecting batteries.

Scan the QR code and watch a short video of cutting and suppression from the cab.

Each of these steps is critical to ensure the stability and safety of the aircraft during a fire or emergency landing. Based on recommendations from IFSTA's *Aircraft Rescue and Fire Fighting*, latest edition, these procedures are key to preventing the spread of fire and protecting occupants and rescuers (IFSTA, 2020).

### Motor Power Reduction

One of the first steps Aircraft Rescue Firefighters must take is to reduce engine power from the cockpit. In emergencies, it is crucial that the engines are shut down to avoid the possibility of a major fire, the spread of combustible materials or even an explosion. Standard procedures indicate that, upon accessing the cab, fire personnel should check the throttle levers and ensure that they are in the fuel cutoff position. In addition, it is important to follow the instructions of aircraft personnel, if available, to ensure that the process is completed safely and effectively (IFSTA, 2020).

# TACTICS AND STRATEGIES FOR AIRCRAFT FIREFIGHTING

## Use of Engine Fire Suppression Systems and APUs

The cockpit is equipped with automatic fire suppression systems for the engines and APU. These systems are essential to contain and extinguish fires before they spread to the rest of the aircraft. Aircraft firefighters should know how to activate these systems from the cockpit in the event that they have not been automatically activated. IFSTA's *Aircraft Rescue and Fire Fighting* book explains that suppression  controls are normally located on the main control panel in the cockpit. When activated, these systems release extinguishing agents such as halon into the affected areas, quickly smothering the fire. In addition, it is critical that firefighters check the status indicators on the panel to confirm that the systems have been activated properly (IFSTA, 2020).

## Battery Power Shutdown

Another crucial task for Aircraft Rescue Firefighters is to disconnect the aircraft's batteries. Batteries are a potential ignition source, especially in situations where electrical systems have been compromised by fire or impact. The

standard procedure involves locating the battery disconnect panel, which is usually located in the cockpit or service compartment. Once identified, firefighters should follow protocol to shut off power to the batteries, thus minimizing the risk of short circuits or secondary electrical fires (IFSTA, 2020).

In short, Aircraft Rescue Firefighters must be fully trained in the procedures for reducing engine power, activating fire suppression systems and disconnecting aircraft batteries. These procedures, detailed in the latest edition of IFSTA's *Aircraft Rescue and Fire Fighting* book, are essential to ensure the safety of both occupants and emergency personnel during a crisis.

### 3.4.2 Primary and Secondary Searches

The primary and secondary search inside the aircraft is critical to the location and rescue of victims. The primary search is conducted quickly to find and evacuate anyone in  immediate danger, while the secondary search is a thorough check of all areas to ensure that there are no trapped or unconscious victims. These searches should be conducted in a systematic manner, dividing the aircraft into sectors and using detection equipment such as thermal cameras to identify victims in low visibility conditions (NFPA 1500, 2022).

Aircraft Rescue Firefighters, as recommended by the FAA and NFPA, should follow a coordinated search pattern to cover all critical areas of the aircraft, beginning with the passenger compartments, cabin, and cargo compartments. Rapid victim identification is essential to minimize injuries and save lives in high-pressure situations (FAA, 2020).

## TACTICS AND STRATEGIES FOR AIRCRAFT FIREFIGHTING

### 3.4.3 Ventilation

Ventilation is an integral part of interior securing in aircraft fires. The purpose of ventilation is to remove smoke and toxic gases from the interior of the aircraft to improve visibility and reduce heat, allowing fire and rescue crews to operate

more safely and efficiently. According to *NFPA 402*, ventilation can be accomplished horizontally, by opening doors and emergency exits to allow smoke to escape, or vertically, by cutting sections of the fuselage or opening roof panels (NFPA, 2022).

The use of positive pressure fans is an effective technique to move air through the aircraft and expel smoke to the outside. This technique must be implemented in a coordinated manner to ensure that escape routes are clear and that hazardous gases do not accumulate in confined areas of the aircraft.

### 3.4.4 Passenger Cabin Fires

Cabin fires are usually the most dangerous due to the density of people and the amount of combustible materials present, such as furniture, electrical systems and baggage. Cabin fires can spread rapidly, affecting the structural integrity of the aircraft and endangering the occupants.

According to *ICAO* and *NFPA*, firefighters should use direct attack techniques to suppress the fire in the passenger cabin as quickly as possible, using AFFF foam or CO2 extinguishers to extinguish the fire and minimize damage. In addition, it is critical to properly ventilate the cabin to remove toxic gases that could incapacitate passengers or rescue personnel (ICAO, 2019).

### 3.4.5 Fires in the Galley

The galley (aircraft galley) is another critical area where fires can start due to electrical equipment or gas leaks. Fires in the galley can be caused by short circuits, equipment malfunctions, or spills of flammable oils and liquids. According to *NFPA 403*, fires in the galley must be quickly suppressed with portable CO2 or dry chemical extinguishers to prevent the fire from spreading to the cabin or other aircraft compartments (NFPA, 2022).

The fire team should ensure that the galley's automatic suppression systems are operational and, in the event of failure, take control using manual extinguishing agents. In addition, it is important to check the electrical and gas systems to ensure that there are no leaks that could rekindle the fire.

### 3.4.6 Bathroom Fires

Aircraft lavatories, although smaller in size, present a significant risk in the event of a fire due to the presence of electrical and chemical cleaning systems. *NFPA 403* and *ICAO* recommend that fires in lavatories be addressed using CO2 extinguishers, which are effective in extinguishing electrical fires and reducing the risk of short circuits. In addition, firefighters should verify that smoke detectors and automatic suppression systems are working properly (ICAO, 2019).

Once the fire is under control, it is essential to ventilate the area to eliminate toxic gases generated by combustible materials in the bathroom, such as plastics and chemicals.

## TACTICS AND STRATEGIES FOR AIRCRAFT FIREFIGHTING

## Conclusion

The tactical priorities of protecting life, stabilizing the incident, and preserving property and the environment form the basis for effective implementation of an IAP in aviation emergencies. These priorities, which are clearly aligned with NFPA, ICAO and FAA regulations, guide the decisions of incident commanders and response teams, ensuring that each operation is focused on protecting people, controlling risk and minimizing damage. The ability to execute these priorities in an organized and flexible manner is critical to the success of any emergency operation in an airport environment.

The aeronautical emergency response sequence is a complex process that requires precise and coordinated execution. Initial assessment, LCANS reporting, spontaneous evacuation assistance and airframe protection are key elements to ensure that the operation is conducted efficiently and that risks to passengers, crew and responders are minimized. Based on international regulations such as NFPA, ICAO and FAA, this structured approach provides clear guidance for IAP implementation in high-pressure and high-risk situations.

Fire control, especially in the Q1 phase, is an essential component of aeronautical emergency response. The ability of aeronautical fire crews to assess the situation, select appropriate extinguishing agents, and apply coordinated control techniques is key to mitigating the impact of fires and protecting both people and infrastructure. Based on NFPA, ICAO, FAA and USAID BHA standards, effective fire control not only saves lives, but also prevents collateral damage and ensures the safety of responders during the response.

The primary search is an essential component in the implementation of the Incident Action Plan in aeronautical emergencies. Its success depends on the speed, systematicity and coordination between the rescue teams and the Incident Commander. By following NFPA, ICAO and FAA regulations, and using advanced technology, aeronautical fire crews can locate and evacuate victims efficiently, minimizing the risk to the people involved. Through proper planning, constant training and the use of standardized protocols, primary search becomes a key element in saving lives during aeronautical emergencies.

Fire suppression, both in the exterior securing (Q2) and interior securing (Q3) phases, is an essential component in the implementation of the Incident Action Plan. Coordination between both phases, proper selection of extinguishing agents and protection of personnel are key factors to ensure a successful operation. By following NFPA, ICAO, FAA and USAID BHA regulations, aeronautical firefighting teams can effectively deal with complex fires, safeguarding lives and minimizing damage to critical infrastructure.

Removal and overhaul, or secondary search, is a crucial phase in aeronautical emergency response. Its objective is to ensure that all victims are rescued and that there are no hidden fire sources that could pose a danger. By following NFPA, ICAO and FAA regulations, and using advanced technology and constant communication, aeronautical fire crews can conduct the secondary search efficiently and safely, minimizing risk and ensuring the effectiveness of the operation.

Exterior securing in aeronautical emergencies is a critical phase involving the containment and extinguishment of a variety of hazardous fires and spills. Success in these operations depends on the correct selection of extinguishing agents and coordination between aeronautical firefighting teams, following international NFPA, ICAO and FAA regulations. By implementing specialized tactics and applying the appropriate technology, teams can effectively and safely control these external hazards, minimizing the risk to aircraft occupants and response personnel.

Emergencies involving landing gear present a unique set of challenges for Aircraft Rescue Firefighters. Overheating brakes, possible tire ignition, and the presence of combustible metals such as magnesium require a specialized response. It is critical that fire crews are equipped with the appropriate extinguishing agents, such as Class D powders, and understand the properties and hazards of the materials involved in these emergencies. The use of nitrogen in tires, the ability to detect and control overheating, and the correct selection of extinguishing agents are key aspects to mitigate these incidents safely and efficiently, following the regulations established by NFPA, IFSTA, and other relevant agencies.

Interior securing in aeronautical emergencies is a critical phase that involves multiple complex tasks, from fire suppression to search and rescue of victims. Following NFPA, ICAO and FAA regulations, Aircraft Rescue Firefighters must act in a coordinated manner, using specialized tools and techniques to cut, suppress and ventilate the interior of the aircraft. The correct implementation of these tactics ensures the safety of both aircraft occupants and responders, minimizing damage and effectively controlling the incident.

# TACTICS AND STRATEGIES FOR AIRCRAFT FIREFIGHTING

## References

IFSTA (2018). *Aircraft Rescue and Fire Fighting*. International Fire Service Training Association.

IFSTA (2020). *Aircraft Rescue and Fire Fighting*. International Fire Service Training Association.

NFPA. (2022). *NFPA 1561: Standard on Emergency Services Incident Management System and Command Safety*. National Fire Protection Association.

ICAO. (2021). *ICAO CRESIA Course on Operational Safety*.

FAA (2020). *Aircraft rescue and firefighting plan (Advisory Circular 150/5210-17C)*. Federal Aviation Administration.

ICAO. (2019). *Airport Services Manual - Part 1: Rescue and Firefighting*. International Civil Aviation Organization.

NFPA. (2022). *NFPA 402: Guide for Aircraft Rescue and Firefighting Operations*. National Fire Protection Association.

NFPA. (2022). *NFPA 403: Standard for Aircraft Rescue and Fire-Fighting Services at Airports*. National Fire Protection Association. Association.

NFPA. (2022). *NFPA 1500: Standard on Fire Department Occupational Safety, Health, and Wellness Program*. National Fire Protection Association.

USAID BHA (2021). *Incident Command System Operations Manual*.

Transportation Safety Board of Canada (TSB) (2005). *Air France Flight 358* Accident Report.

NTSB. (2014). *Asiana Airlines Flight 214 Accident Report*.

NTSB. (1990). *Accident Report: United Airlines Flight 232*.

*NTSB. (2008).* Accident Report: British Airways Flight 268.

# CHAPTER 4

# EVALUATING PROGRESS

# TACTICS AND STRATEGIES FOR AIRCRAFT FIREFIGHTING

## INTRODUCTION

Progress evaluation is an essential phase in the management of aeronautical emergencies. This process involves continuously monitoring the actions being taken during an incident response to ensure that the objectives established in the Incident Action Plan (IAP) are met and that operations remain safe, coordinated, and effective. The ability to properly assess progress is crucial to adjust tactics and strategies in real time, allowing for a more adaptive and effective response to complex and evolving emergencies.

According to *National Fire Protection Association* (NFPA) and *International Civil Aviation Organization (ICAO)* regulations, continuous assessment of operations is key to ensuring that resources are being optimally utilized and that risks to both responders and aircraft occupants are minimized (NFPA 1561, 2022; ICAO, 2019). This chapter focuses on the principles and methods of progress assessment in the context of aeronautical rescue and firefighting operations, based on international regulations and best practices developed by leaders in operational safety.

### Importance of Continuous Evaluation

Under the Incident Command System (ICS), progress assessment allows incident commanders and response teams to maintain rigorous control over the evolution of the event. Each phase of the response, from fire suppression to passenger evacuation and critical infrastructure protection, must be constantly monitored to ensure that tactical objectives are met. *According to NFPA 1561* and the *FAA*, continuous assessment includes such things as reviewing the effectiveness of extinguishing agents, the safety of evacuation routes, the structural stability of the aircraft, and the condition of fuel and electrical systems (NFPA 1561, 2022; FAA, 2020).

The assessment focuses not only on tactical and technical aspects, but also on the welfare and safety of the response personnel. The incident commander must constantly monitor the physical and mental state of Aircraft Rescue Firefighters, ensuring that they are not exposed to unnecessary risk and that relief procedures are implemented when necessary. This is especially important in prolonged or high-intensity situations, where fatigue can compromise the effectiveness of operations and jeopardize the safety of equipment (IFSTA, 2020).

## Evaluation Methods

There are several methods for assessing progress during an aviation emergency, and these should be applied continuously and systematically. One of the most common methods is the use of **periodic status reports**, in which the leaders of each team provide regular updates on the status of their operations. These reports should include details on progress in suppressing the fire, locating and evacuating victims, and any changes in incident conditions. Situation reports allow the Incident commander to make informed decisions and tactical adjustments in real time (IFSTA, 2020).

Another key method is the **use of real-time monitoring technology**, such as thermal cameras and drones, which provide fire crews with a more accurate view of the incident and allow for the detection of any residual fire hot spots or hidden heat areas. According to *ICAO* and *NFPA* regulations, these technological tools are essential for accurate assessments and reducing the risk of reignition or fire spread (ICAO, 2019; NFPA 403, 2022).

## Adjustments and Decisions Based on Evaluation

Once information is gathered through the assessment methods, it is critical that the Incident commander be prepared to make adjustments to the action plan as necessary. These adjustments may involve redeploying resources, relocating firefighting equipment, modifying fire attack tactics, or implementing additional safety measures. The ability to make quick, well-informed decisions based on assessment of progress is a key indicator of success in aviation emergency management (FAA, 2020).

For example, if during the assessment it is discovered that the fire is beginning to spread to an unaffected part of the aircraft, the Incident commander may decide to redirect additional resources to that area and activate automatic or manual extinguishing systems. Similarly, if evacuation routes are found to have become unsafe due to smoke or debris accumulation, assessment of progress would allow escape routes to be adjusted and ensure the safety of passengers and response personnel (IFSTA, 2020).

## Documentation and Lessons Learned

A crucial part of the progress evaluation is the documentation of all actions and decisions taken during the incident. This documentation not only provides a detailed record of what happened, but is also essential for subsequent analysis of the incident and identification of lessons learned. According to *NFPA* and *FAA*, this documentation process is vital for improving future training and adjusting operating procedures for future similar incidents (NFPA 1561, 2022; FAA, 2020).

The post-incident analysis should include a detailed review of response times, effectiveness of extinguishing tactics, coordination between different teams, and any issues that arose during operations. Lessons learned through this analysis should be integrated into future training and drill plans, ensuring that aeronautical firefighting teams are better prepared to deal with emergencies in the future (IFSTA, 2020).

## 4.1 Importance of Continuous Assessment

Continuous evaluation is an essential part of the aviation emergency management process. This phase ensures that action plans are properly executed and that decisions made are adjusted to changing incident conditions. In dynamic situations such as aircraft emergencies, continuous assessment allows incident commanders to monitor progress in real time and adjust tactics to ensure effectiveness and safety. Evaluation not only focuses on tactical aspects, but also assesses resource utilization, personnel safety, and outcomes against strategic and operational objectives established at the beginning of the incident (NFPA 1561, 2022; IFSTA, 2020).

The continuous evaluation process is not static. It requires the incident commander and response team leaders to conduct regular assessments of progress and needs for adjustment of the Incident Action Plan (IAP). In this regard, evaluation not only ensures that initial objectives are achieved, but also allows strategies and tactics to be adapted as the emergency evolves. According to *National Fire Protection Association* (NFPA) regulations and *International Civil Aviation Organization (ICAO)* recommendations, continuous assessment is key to ensure an effective and coordinated response in aviation emergencies (NFPA 403, 2022; ICAO, 2019).

### 4.1.1 Evaluation Objectives

The main objective of continuous evaluation is to ensure that the actions implemented are effective and in line with the objectives of the IAP. The evaluation also seeks to identify potential weaknesses in the initial strategy and provide real-time feedback to the response teams. According *to NFPA 1561*, the objectives of the evaluation include:

- **Monitor the effectiveness of extinguishing agents**: Verify that the resources deployed, such as the use of foam or $CO_2$ extinguishers, are achieving the expected results in suppressing the fire.
- **Review the safety of rescue operations**: Ensure that evacuation and rescue procedures are being carried out safely and efficiently, and that escape routes are clear and accessible.
- **Evaluate the use of resources**: Ensure that resources, both human and material, are being used efficiently and that sufficient resources are available to continue operations (NFPA 403, 2022).

In addition, the assessment aims to ensure the safety of the personnel involved in the operation. This includes reviewing the fatigue of firefighters and rescue personnel, as well as the condition of their personal protective equipment (PPE) to prevent further injury or complications during the incident (IFSTA, 2020).

### 4.1.2 Difference between Evaluation and Supervision

Although assessment and supervision are closely related, it is important to differentiate between them. **Supervision** involves the continuous observation of operations to ensure that procedures are being followed and that responders are working in accordance with established regulations. It is an ongoing process and focuses on ensuring compliance with safety standards and operational protocols. Supervision is usually performed by team leaders or shift leaders who report directly to the Incident commander (NFPA 1500, 2022).

On the other hand, **evaluation** is a broader process that involves a detailed analysis of the results obtained in terms of the established objectives. Evaluation focuses not only on compliance with procedures, but also on the analysis of the effectiveness of the tactics and strategies implemented. In addition, evaluation includes data collection to identify areas for improvement, which can influence future tactical and strategic decisions. In summary, while monitoring ensures that operations remain within safety limits, evaluation seeks to improve the overall efficiency and effectiveness of the action plan (NFPA 1561, 2022; IFSTA, 2020).

### 4.1.3 Frequency of Evaluations

The frequency of assessments during an incident depends largely on the nature and complexity of the incident. In aviation emergencies, assessments should be conducted at regular intervals, depending on the rate at which incident conditions evolve. According to *NFPA 1561*, assessments should be conducted as soon as new tactics are implemented, when major milestones in the operation are achieved, or when environmental conditions change significantly (NFPA 1561, 2022).

In addition, the frequency of assessments may depend on the type of incident. In situations where the fire has been contained, but the risk of re-ignition remains, assessments should be more frequent to monitor the affected areas and prevent the fire from spreading again. In emergencies involving hazardous substances or where there are additional risks such as structural collapses, assessments should also be conducted more frequently to ensure that responders are operating safely (ICAO, 2019).

Assessments should also be conducted after each shift change or personnel relief, ensuring that incoming teams are fully briefed on the current status of the incident and the tactics implemented. In protracted situations, continuous assessment allows incident commanders to adjust resource use and better manage personnel fatigue, ensuring operations remain safe and effective over time (IFSTA, 2020).

## 4.2 Tools and Methods to Evaluate Progress

Continuous assessment of progress during an aviation emergency is critical to ensure that the actions and strategies deployed are aligned with the objectives established in the Incident Action Plan (IAP). To conduct this assessment effectively, incident commanders and response teams need tools and methods that allow them to measure, monitor and adjust operations in real time. International regulations, such as those of the *National Fire Protection Association* (NFPA), the *International Civil Aviation Organization (ICAO),* and the *Federal Aviation Administration* (FAA), emphasize the importance of using key performance indicators (KPIs) and advanced real-time monitoring technology to assess progress and make informed decisions during the incident (NFPA 1561, 2022; ICAO, 2019).

## TACTICS AND STRATEGIES FOR AIRCRAFT FIREFIGHTING

### 4.2.1 Key Performance Indicators (KPIs)

**Key performance indicators (KPIs)** are fundamental metrics to measure the success or progress of an emergency operation. In the context of aviation emergencies, KPIs help evaluate critical aspects such as the efficiency of fire suppression tactics, response time, safety of emergency personnel, and effectiveness in evacuating aircraft occupants. According to *NFPA 1561* regulations, KPIs must not only be aligned with the tactical and strategic objectives of the IAP, but must also be measurable, specific, and time-specific, allowing for continuous and effective monitoring (NFPA 1561, 2022).

Some of the most common KPIs used in assessing progress during aviation emergencies include:

- **Initial response time**: This KPI measures the time it takes for the fire team to arrive at the incident scene from the time the alert is received. According to *ICAO* and *NFPA 403*, the ability to respond quickly to an emergency is critical to reduce the spread of fire and protect human life. Standards suggest that rescue teams should be on the scene within three minutes of alarm activation (ICAO, 2019; NFPA 403, 2022).
- **Fire suppression effectiveness**: This KPI refers to the ability of fire crews to efficiently contain and extinguish the fire. Factors such as the amount of foam or water used, the time required to extinguish the fire and the coordination between teams are critical to measure success in this area. ICAO document 9137 establishes control times and suppression times in standard fire situations in the critical area of an aircraft, these correspond to 1 minute of control Q1 and 1 minute of suppression Q2, this of course, under optimal conditions or as I call them *"rosy"*; NFPA 403 establishes an additional time of 10 minutes for interior attacks from category 4 to 10 and 5 minutes for category 3, leaving categories 1 and 2 without interior attacks due to the

size of their aircraft, this phase is called Q3, and includes the amount of water that must be guaranteed for each airport category in order to perform interior attacks in a given time, periodic situation reports and post-incident analysis help to evaluate this KPI (IFSTA, 2020).

- **Number of victims safely evacuated**: This KPI measures the number of people who have been evacuated safely and within the allotted time. A quick and efficient evacuation is a key indicator of the success of the rescue operation. According to *FAA* recommendations, this KPI may also include the percentage of passengers rescued compared to the total number of aircraft occupants (FAA, 2020).

- **Safety of response personnel**: The protection of Aircraft Rescue Firefighters and emergency personnel is a priority at any incident. This KPI monitors the number of injuries or incidents among personnel, reflecting the effectiveness of safety procedures and risk management. *NFPA 1500* establishes clear guidelines on how to measure this KPI, including analysis of the frequency and severity of injuries (NFPA 1500, 2022).

KPIs provide a quantitative basis for assessing progress and allow for real-time adjustments. By monitoring these indicators, incident commanders can make more informed decisions and ensure that resources are optimally allocated.

### 4.2.2 Use of Technology for Real-Time Monitoring

The **use of real-time monitoring technology** is another crucial tool for assessing progress during an aviation emergency. Technological advances allow responders to obtain up-to-date and accurate information about incident conditions, which is vital to making quick and effective decisions. According to *NFPA* regulations and *IFSTA* recommendations, the use of technologies such as thermal cameras, drones, and advanced communication systems has significantly improved the ability of aeronautical fire crews to assess progress in real time (NFPA 403, 2022; IFSTA, 2020).

Some of the most used technologies for real-time monitoring include:

- **Thermal cameras**: These cameras allow fire crews to detect hot spots and high-risk areas that are not visible to the naked eye. During an aircraft fire, thermal cameras can identify hot spots in the fuselage, engines, or cargo compartments, which helps responders prioritize specific areas for fire suppression. According to the *FAA*, the use of thermal cameras can also help detect residual fires that might go undetected during a visual inspection (FAA, 2020).

- **Drones**: Drones equipped with high-resolution cameras and thermal sensors provide an aerial view of the incident, allowing incident commanders to assess the situation from different angles and monitor the progress of operations without putting firefighters at risk. This technology is especially useful in areas that are difficult to access or when the incident is unfolding over a wide location, such as on the runway or in maintenance hangars. *ICAO* has recommended the use of drones in emergency response operations because of their ability to provide real-time information and improve decision making (ICAO, 2019).

- **Advanced communication systems**: Digital radio and communication systems allow for seamless coordination between different response teams. These systems ensure that incident commanders receive constant updates on the progress of operations and can adjust tactics as needed. Effective communication is essential to ensure the safety of all involved and maximize the efficiency of operations. According to *NFPA 1561*, implementing robust communication systems is key to success in managing complex emergencies (NFPA 1561, 2022).

The use of these technologies significantly improves the ability of aeronautical firefighting teams to continuously assess progress and make informed decisions in real time. In addition, these tools enable faster and more accurate response, which is essential for mitigating risks in highly complex emergencies.

### 4.3 Staff Performance Evaluation

The evaluation of personnel performance during emergency operations is a fundamental part of the crisis management process. In the context of aeronautical emergencies, where Aircraft Rescue Firefighters must perform under extreme conditions, continuous performance evaluation at both the individual and team levels ensures that the objectives set forth in the Incident Action Plan (IAP) are met. In addition, a thorough review of performance allows areas for improvement to be identified and operational strategies for future incidents to be refined. This chapter, based on *National Fire Protection Association* (NFPA), *International Civil Aviation Organization (ICAO),* and *Federal Aviation Administration* (FAA) regulations, explores the tools and methods used to evaluate personnel performance during and after an aeronautical emergency (NFPA 1500, 2022; ICAO, 2019).

### 4.3.1 Individual and Team Performance

The performance of response personnel in an aviation emergency is a critical factor in the success of operations. Individual performance evaluation focuses on measuring each firefighter's ability to fulfill his or her specific role within the team, while team performance evaluation focuses on the cohesion, coordination, and overall effectiveness of the response groups.

### Individual Performance

Individual performance evaluation is based on several key factors, such as technical ability, decision-making under pressure, and proper

use of personal protective equipment (PPE). According to *NFPA
1500*, Aircraft Rescue Firefighters must be evaluated on their ability
to correctly apply firefighting techniques, operate emergency control
systems, and safely respond to changing incident conditions (NFPA
1500, 2022). This evaluation also considers compliance with
procedures established in the IAP, such as extinguisher handling,
application of AFFF foam on two- and three-dimensional fires, and
the ability to shut down critical aircraft systems, such as fuel or
electrical power (IFSTA, 2020).

A critical aspect of individual assessment is the firefighter's ability to
adapt to dynamic situations. During an emergency, changes in fire
conditions, the emergence of new hazards, or the need to evacuate
injured passengers require each team member to respond quickly and
accurately. Incident commanders should document how each
firefighter manages these changes and whether his or her actions
contribute to operational objectives. After Action Review (AAR)
also plays a crucial role in this assessment, allowing firefighters to
reflect on their performance and learn from their experiences
(USAID BHA, 2021), this topic we will address in more detail in
Chapter 5.

**Team Performance**

The success of an emergency operation depends largely on the
cohesion and effectiveness of the aeronautical firefighting team. The
evaluation of team performance focuses on the group's ability to
work in a coordinated and efficient manner under the Incident
commander's directives. *NFPA 1561* states that teams should be
evaluated in terms of their ability to implement fire suppression
tactics, conduct evacuations safely and effectively, and coordinate
with other response teams and emergency services (NFPA 1561,
2022).

Communication within the team is an essential component of its
performance. According to *ICAO*, teams that maintain clear and
continuous communication are more effective in performing

complex and hazardous tasks, such as aircraft ventilation or fire suppression in engines and cargo compartments (ICAO, 2019). Teams should also be evaluated on their ability to adapt to changes in the incident, such as the spread of fire or the emergence of new hazards, and their ability to coordinate with other teams or external institutions involved in the response.

In addition, the team's ability to meet **key performance indicators (KPIs)**, such as response time, number of victims evacuated, and effective fire suppression, is a direct reflection of its performance. Reviewing these KPIs during and after the incident provides a quantitative basis for evaluating the success of the team's operations (NFPA 1500, 2022).

### 4.3.2 Personnel Safety

Personnel safety is a priority in any emergency operation, and assessment of this aspect is crucial to ensure that procedures are conducted safely and without compromising the physical or mental integrity of firefighters. According to NFPA 1500, incident commanders must conduct ongoing assessments of personnel safety during all phases of the incident. This includes monitoring the proper use of personal protective equipment (PPE), ensuring that tactics employed minimize risks, and ensuring that relief teams are activated in a timely manner to avoid fatigue (NFPA 1500, 2022).

### Proper Use of Personal Protective Equipment (PPE)

Proper use of PPE is a key safety measure that should be evaluated at all levels of the firefighting team. According to the FAA, firefighters should be evaluated on their ability to properly use their protective suits, helmets, gloves, and self-contained breathing apparatus (SCBA). Protective equipment should be inspected before and after each operation to ensure that it meets safety standards and has not been compromised during the incident (FAA, 2020). Incidents of equipment failure or improper use should be documented and corrected through additional training or improvements in operating procedures.

## Staff Fatigue Assessment

Fatigue is one of the greatest risks to personnel safety during prolonged or high-intensity operations. According to *NFPA 1561*, incident commanders must constantly monitor the physical and mental state of firefighters and activate relief protocols when necessary. Regular assessments identify early signs of fatigue, which helps prevent accidents or critical errors that could compromise the safety of equipment or the effectiveness of the operation (NFPA 1561, 2022).

Implementation of **regular breaks** and rotation of equipment in long duration emergencies are recommended strategies to avoid extreme fatigue. Assessment of personnel fatigue should be part of ongoing incident monitoring, with emphasis on the mental health and physical well-being of Aircraft Rescue Firefighters.

## 4.4 Assessment of Resource Effectiveness

In aeronautical emergency operations, the effectiveness of the resources deployed can make the difference between success and failure in the response. The ability of fire crews to properly utilize available resources, including equipment, materials, water and foam, is crucial to safely contain the fire and rescue the people on board. Assessing the effectiveness of resources is an essential part of incident management and should be conducted on an ongoing basis throughout the response process. Following *National Fire Protection Association* (NFPA), *International Civil Aviation Organization (ICAO),* and *Federal Aviation Administration* (FAA) regulations, resources should be evaluated in terms of their proper use, supply capability, and resupply methods (NFPA 403, 2022; ICAO, 2019).

# TACTICS AND STRATEGIES FOR AIRCRAFT FIREFIGHTING

## 4.4.1 Proper Use of Equipment and Materials

Proper use of equipment and materials is critical to the effectiveness of aeronautical emergency response. Aeronautical fire crews are trained to operate a variety of specialized devices, such as firefighting vehicles (ARFF), cutting tools, ventilation systems, and thermal cameras. Evaluating the effectiveness of the use of this equipment involves reviewing how it was used during the incident and whether its deployment contributed to meeting the objectives of the Incident Action Plan (IAP).

The *International Fire Service Training Association's* (IFSTA) *Aircraft Rescue and Fire Fighting* stresses the importance of firefighters understanding the capabilities and limitations of each piece of equipment, ensuring that they are used safely and efficiently during an emergency (IFSTA, 2020). The assessment should include analysis of how quickly the equipment was deployed, how effective it was in suppressing the fire, and whether there were any malfunctions or delays in operation. In addition, maintenance procedures should be reviewed to ensure that equipment is in optimal condition before the next incident.

For example, in the use of ARFF vehicles, the performance evaluation should focus on the team's ability to arrive at the incident site in the *ICAO-recommended* time of three minutes or less from alarm activation, as well as its ability to effectively and accurately apply AFFF foam to contain and extinguish the fire (ICAO, 2019). Also, personal protective equipment (PPE), including firefighter suits, self-contained breathing apparatus (SCBA) and cutting tools, should be evaluated to ensure that they were used properly and provided adequate protection to response personnel.

## 4.4.2 Water and Foam Supply Capability

Water and foam supply capability is another key aspect in assessing the effectiveness of resources during an aircraft emergency. The success of the firefighting operation depends largely on the availability and timely deployment of these extinguishing agents. According to *NFPA 403*, Aircraft Rescue Firefighters must have access to sufficient supplies of water and foam to deal with large fires, such as those involving fuel spills on runways or three-dimensional engine and airframe fires (NFPA 403, 2022).

Aqueous film-forming foam (AFFF) is the primary extinguishing agent used on aircraft fuel fires. To evaluate the effectiveness of its use, incident commanders should review factors such as the amount of foam applied, how quickly it was deployed, and whether it was sufficient to smother the flames and prevent reignition. In addition, it must be ensured that ARFF vehicles and automatic extinguishing systems at airport facilities are well stocked and ready for use at a moment's notice (FAA, 2020).

In prolonged or high intensity incidents, water supply capacity should also be evaluated. Water sources should be available in the vicinity of the incident site, either through hydrants or water tankers, to ensure a constant supply during the extinguishing operation. If a deficiency in supply is identified, improvements to water and foam storage and distribution systems should be implemented for future emergencies.

### 4.4.3 Replenishment Methods (Sustained, Rapid and Point of Replenishment)

Adequate water and foam replenishment during an emergency is critical to ensure that fire crews have the necessary resources to continue the firefighting operation without interruption. There are several methods of resupply, and the evaluation of their effectiveness depends on the type of incident and the availability of resources at the scene.

- **Sustained replenishment**: This method involves maintaining a constant flow of water and foam from a nearby source, such as hydrants or groundwater systems. It is ideal for situations where the fire extends over a long period of time and a constant amount of extinguishing agents is required. According to *NFPA*, sustained refueling is especially effective at large airports where a robust infrastructure for continuous water and foam supply is available (NFPA 403, 2022).

- **Rapid Refueling**: In situations where access to water and foam resources is limited, rapid refueling allows ARFF vehicles to travel to a nearby point to refuel and return to the incident site. This method is ideal for emergencies that require rapid intervention but are not  extended in time. Rapid refueling points should be strategically located near risk areas and be easily accessible to firefighting vehicles (IFSTA, 2020), it is in this type of refueling that we position water supply pools and tankers that are outside of the operational calculations, In our case, at the International Airport "Alfonso Bonilla Aragón" in the city of Cali, Colombia, we have 1 large capacity machine of old destined ONLY and EXCLUSIVELY as a tanker truck, the M-15 of 4.000 gallons of capacity (scan the code to see the M-15 operating), in addition to this, we have 1 water storage pool of 3,000 gallons transported in the M-15 itself to be deployed and used in emergencies that warrant it.

- **Refueling Point**: In large incidents or prolonged situations, dedicated refueling points may be established where vehicles and equipment can refuel water and foam without interrupting suppression operations. These points should be equipped with sufficient resources to meet the demands of the operation. The evaluation of this method focuses on the speed and efficiency of the refueling process, as well as the ability to maintain the flow of operations without interruption.

This is the least efficient of the refueling methods, as there is usually only a fixed gravity refueling tank, subway tanks to be used by suction in the airport infrastructure, and finally, fixed hydrants established in fuel storage tanks that provide large capacity, any of the 3 ways requires the displacement  of RFF trucks to these points for the respective refueling, which will always result in increased times and the need for non-simultaneous and coordinated attacks so that not all trucks change their status to (unavailable) due to lack of extinguishing agent.

The ability to establish and maintain efficient refueling is critical to the continuity of firefighting operations and should be evaluated at the conclusion of the incident. *FAA* and *NFPA* recommendations suggest that airports periodically review their refueling capabilities and conduct drills to ensure that systems are prepared for real emergencies (FAA, 2020; NFPA 403, 2022).

### 4.5 Review and Adjustment of the Incident Action Plan (IAP)

The management of an aeronautical emergency is not a static process; as the incident progresses, conditions can change rapidly and unexpectedly. This makes continuous review and adjustment of the Incident Action Plan (IAP) a critical element for a successful operation. The IAP must be dynamic, allowing for adaptations based on the evolution of the emergency, available resources, and additional risks that may arise. According to *National Fire Protection Association* (NFPA), *International Civil Aviation Organization (ICAO),* and *Federal Aviation Administration* (FAA) regulations, the ability to

adjust the IAP in real time ensures an effective and safe response
(NFPA 1561, 2022; ICAO, 2019).

### 4.5.1 Real Time Feedback

**Real-time feedback** is a critical process in the review and
adjustment of the IAP. It consists of continuously gathering
information from the incident scene and from ongoing operations
to identify if current tactics are effective or if modifications are
needed. Incident commanders should be in constant communication
with team leaders and monitor progress through periodic status
reports. Real-time assessment allows leaders to detect problems,
such as insufficient resources, fire spread to unanticipated areas, or
the emergence of new threats, such as fuel leaks or structural
collapses (NFPA 403, 2022).

The *Incident Command System* (ICS) facilitates real-time feedback
through a constant flow of information between the diverse levels of
command and the operational teams. According to *NFPA 1561*
regulations, each task force must provide regular reports to the
Incident Commander on the status of their operations. This
information includes the effectiveness of tactics employed, the
condition of evacuation routes, the availability of resources, and any
significant changes in incident conditions (NFPA 1561, 2022).

Technology plays a vital role in real-time feedback. The use of
thermal cameras, drones, and digital monitoring systems allows
commanders to get a more accurate picture of the situation on the
ground. This visual information, combined with equipment reports,
helps identify areas where the IAP may need immediate adjustments
(IFSTA, 2020).

### 4.5.2 Adjustment Procedures

Once real-time feedback has been received, it is critical to have **clear
procedures for adjusting** the IAP. The Incident Commander is

responsible for evaluating the information received and making quick decisions to modify tactics, reallocate resources or introduce new safety measures. According to *FAA* regulations, any adjustments should be immediately communicated to all response teams to ensure that the new approach is implemented in a coordinated and effective manner (FAA, 2020).

**Adjustments to the EPI may include:**

- **Reallocation of resources**: If an assessment reveals that the fire has spread to an unanticipated area, the Incident commander may reassign additional firefighting teams to that area, while ensuring that other critical areas are not left unprotected.
- **Changes to evacuation routes**: If an escape route becomes unsafe due to fire spread or collapse of structures, the EPI should be updated to redirect teams and victims to safer alternate routes (NFPA 403, 2022).
- **Modification of extinguishing tactics**: If the AFFF foam is not being effective in suppressing the fire, the Incident commander may decide to switch to alternative extinguishing agents, such as carbon dioxide or dry chemical powder, depending on the type of fire (IFSTA, 2020).

It is crucial that any adjustments to the IAP are followed by a verification process to ensure that the new strategy is working as planned. The ability to adjust the IAP in an agile and effective manner is one of the cornerstones of a successful response to aviation emergencies.

### 4.5.3 Real Cases of Adaptation to the AIP

There are numerous cases where the ability of incident commanders to **adapt the IAP** has been key to the success of the operation. One prominent example is the handling of the fire on Asiana Airlines

## TACTICS AND STRATEGIES FOR AIRCRAFT
## FIREFIGHTING

Flight 214 at San Francisco International Airport in 2013. Initially, fire crews deployed foam to suppress the fire caused by a crash landing. However, upon receiving reports that the fire was spreading into the cargo compartments, the Incident commander adjusted the AIP, redirecting additional resources to contain the fire in that area and using alternative extinguishing agents. This quick adaptation was crucial to control the fire and prevent a major catastrophe (NTSB, 2014).

Another example is the crash of British Airways Flight 268 at Heathrow Airport in 2008. During the rescue operation, it was discovered that the aircraft's automatic evacuation systems were not functioning properly. The Incident commander quickly modified the AIP to activate additional rescue teams and create new evacuation routes. This timely change allowed all passengers to be evacuated safely with no fatalities (NTSB, 2008).

These cases underscore the importance of continuous assessment and the ability to make effective adjustments to the IAP. Flexibility in incident management, combined with a robust real-time feedback system, allows response teams to adapt to changing conditions and improve the chances of success.

### 4.6 Documents and Progress Reports

Documentation and progress reporting are critical components of aviation emergency management. Maintaining an accurate record of assessments, decisions and actions taken during an incident is essential to ensure continuity of operations, evidence-based decision making and continuous improvement of operating procedures. According to *National Fire Protection Association* (NFPA), *International Civil Aviation Organization (ICAO)*, and *Federal Aviation Administration* (FAA) regulations, proper documentation management allows for analysis of performance and effectiveness of resources used, and is a valuable tool for post-incident analysis and future training (NFPA 1561, 2022; ICAO, 2019).

# TACTICS AND STRATEGIES FOR AIRCRAFT FIREFIGHTING

## 4.6.1 Record of Evaluations Taken

The **record of assessments made** during an emergency is critical for monitoring progress and making real-time decisions. These assessments include status reports provided by team leaders, strategic decisions by the Incident Commander, and resource use assessments. **NFPA 1561** states that all major decisions should be documented to allow clear tracking of actions and their effectiveness (NFPA 1561, 2022).

A detailed record of evaluations should include the following elements:

- **Incident Status**: An updated description of the situation, including the extent of the fire, location of victims, and status of rescue operations. This information should be recorded periodically to provide a clear picture of how the incident is evolving, within the incident command system process is the SCI 201 (Incident Summary) form.
- **Decision making**: Every strategic decision made by the Incident commander should be documented, including the reasons behind the decisions and the expected outcomes. This is crucial to later evaluate if the decisions made were the right ones and to identify areas for improvement in future operations, in incidents that have escalated to fixed mode, in which a solid command is already deployed, it is planned under the SCI 202 form (incident action plan), which establishes the planning of objectives and strategies, tactics, resources and the organizational structure that will enter into the incident, The operations section records all its tactical assignments in the SCI 204 form, which must be in accordance with what was planned in the AIP and must have the appropriate records of modifications due to operational changes.
- **Use of resources**: The use of all resources deployed during the incident, including extinguishing vehicles, AFFF foam, water, and specialized equipment should be recorded. In

addition, an assessment of whether the resources were sufficient or if there were any limitations that impacted the effectiveness of the operation should be included (IFSTA, 2020), within the incident command system process is the SCI 211 form (recording and control of resources).

This log is a valuable tool for post-incident analysis, as it provides a detailed basis for evaluating the effectiveness of operations and for making adjustments to emergency procedures.

### 4.6.2 Intermediate Reports

**Interim reports** are reports generated during the course of an incident that allow incident commanders and other key players to continuously monitor operations. These reports should be shared throughout the chain of command to ensure that all involved are aware of the situation and can effectively coordinate their efforts. According to *NFPA* and *FAA* recommendations, interim reports are essential to maintain clear and fluid communication, both within response teams and with external institutions that may be involved in the incident (NFPA 1500, 2022; FAA, 2020).

It should be noted that in chapter 3 we saw the initial **LCANS** reporting model, throughout the incident we will use the **CAN** report (conditions, actions and needs) to ensure the proper flow of information to the strategic level of the incident, in addition to this **CAN** report, we will use the **RECOP** (personnel recount), to ensure safety when conditions change or there is a new assignment, this **RECOP** must be captured with execution time on the command board in an incident that has escalated to fixed mode.

**An interim report should include:**

- **Current Conditions**: A detailed description of fire conditions, including any significant changes that have occurred since the last report. This may include changes in fire spread, adverse weather conditions, or new hazards that have arisen.

- **Progress of operations**: An assessment of how rescue and fire suppression operations have progressed, highlighting successes achieved and any obstacles encountered. This allows incident commanders to adjust tactics as necessary to improve the effectiveness of the operation (IFSTA, 2020).

- **Resource availability**: A report on the amount of resources currently available, including the status of ARFF vehicles, the amount of AFFF foam and water remaining, and the status of response personnel. This helps to anticipate whether additional resources will be needed and to organize resupply in a timely manner (ICAO, 2019).

- **Recommendations and adjustments**: If problems or limitations in current operations have been identified, interim reports should include recommendations to adjust the Incident Action Plan (IAP). This may involve reallocating resources, modifying extinguishment tactics, or adjusting evacuation routes.

### Importance of Documentation for Continuous Improvement

Detailed documentation during an incident is not only crucial to the management of the emergency itself, but also plays an essential role in the continuous improvement of operating procedures. By reviewing post-incident documents and progress reports, emergency operations leaders can identify which tactics and decisions were effective and which areas need adjustment. This allows emergency response organizations to refine their procedures and improve personnel training (NFPA 1561, 2022).

A detailed analysis of interim reports also provides valuable information for the development of drills and training exercises. By basing these exercises on actual incidents and the challenges faced during those events, fire crews can better prepare for future incidents, ensuring that lessons learned are applied in the field.

## 4.7 Impact and Outcome Measurement

In aeronautical emergency management, **measuring impact and outcome** is essential to evaluate the overall effectiveness of rescue and firefighting operations. Comparison between the objectives set forth in the Incident Action Plan (IAP) and the results achieved allows incident commanders, Aircraft Rescue Firefighters and operations leaders to understand the degree of success of the tactics implemented and to adjust future procedures. In addition, the impact on infrastructure and the environment is a critical aspect that must be evaluated to identify the long-term consequences of emergency operations. Regulations from the *National Fire Protection Association* (NFPA), the *International Civil Aviation Organization (ICAO),* and the *Federal Aviation Administration* (FAA) provide clear frameworks for conducting these assessments, ensuring that both immediate outcomes and long-term repercussions are considered in the incident review (NFPA 403, 2022; ICAO, 2019).

### 4.7.1 Comparison between Objectives and Results

The first step in **measuring impact and outcome** is to compare the objectives set at the beginning of the incident with the results obtained at the end of operations. This comparison identifies whether the objectives of the IAP were effectively achieved or if there were significant deviations that require further analysis.

According to *NFPA 1561* regulations, objectives should be specific, measurable, achievable, realistic and time-bound (SMART), which facilitates their comparison with outcomes. The main objectives in an aviation emergency generally include rapid fire suppression, safe evacuation of all aircraft occupants, protection of airport infrastructure, and mitigation of environmental hazards (NFPA 1561, 2022). Key performance indicators (KPIs) used to measure results include:

- **Response time:** One of the most important KPIs is the time it takes for fire crews to reach the incident site and start fire suppression operations. *ICAO* regulations state that response time should be less than three minutes from alarm activation, which is critical to minimize fire spread and save lives (ICAO, 2019).

- **Number of victims rescued**: The safety of the aircraft occupants is the primary objective. The related KPI measures how many people were evacuated safely and within the estimated time. Post-incident reports should compare the number of passengers rescued to total occupants to determine the effectiveness of rescue operations.

- **Fire suppression effectiveness**: This KPI measures how quickly and effectively the fire was suppressed, and whether resources such as AFFF foam and water were used appropriately. The analysis includes the amount of resources used and whether they needed to be replenished during the operation (NFPA 403, 2022).

## 4.7.2 Impact on Infrastructure and the Environment

In addition to the evaluation of operational performance, it is essential to measure the **impact on** airport **infrastructure** and the **environment**. Emergency operations, especially aeronautical fires, can cause damage to airport infrastructure such as runways, hangars and control systems. In addition, the use of large quantities of water and extinguishing foam can have negative effects on the environment if not handled properly.

### Impact on Infrastructure

The infrastructure impact assessment involves analyzing the damage caused during the incident and the firefighting operations. According to the *FAA*, it is necessary to inspect structural damage to runways and affected aircraft, as well as any damage to communications systems or vehicles used during the operation (FAA, 2020). In addition, the implementation of automatic fire suppression systems and the use of materials such as AFFF foam can impact the integrity of the infrastructure, requiring post-incident review and maintenance.

An example of this was observed during the crash of British Airways Flight 268 at Heathrow Airport in 2008, where fire suppression operations caused damage to nearby runways and hangars, requiring significant repairs and re-evaluation of AFFF foam use procedures (NTSB, 2008). Post-incident reports identified the need to adjust procedures to minimize the impact on infrastructure while ensuring effective fire suppression.

### Impact on the Environment

**Environmental impact** is another crucial factor to assess following a large-scale incident. The use of large volumes of water and AFFF foam can cause contamination of soil and nearby water bodies. AFFF foam, in particular, contains fluorinated compounds (PFAS) that have been of increasing concern due to their persistence in the environment and their potential to contaminate groundwater sources.

*NFPA 403* and *ICAO* recommend that airports implement environmental management plans that include the responsible use of extinguishing chemicals and the proper containment of waste generated during emergency operations (NFPA 403, 2022; ICAO, 2019). The ability to properly contain and dispose of hazardous waste, including foam debris and spilled fuels, is essential to minimize environmental impact.

# TACTICS AND STRATEGIES FOR AIRCRAFT
# FIREFIGHTING

A recent case that illustrates the importance of assessing environmental impact is the crash of Asiana Airlines Flight 214 at San Francisco International Airport in 2013.

If you want to see more of this accident, scan the QR code.

Following the incident, environmental impact assessments were conducted due to the extensive use of AFFF foam, leading to the implementation of new waste management and contamination mitigation practices in future emergencies (NTSB, 2014).

# TACTICS AND STRATEGIES FOR AIRCRAFT FIREFIGHTING

## Conclusion

Progress evaluation is an essential component of aviation emergency response, and its effective implementation can make the difference between success and failure in managing an incident. Through continuous evaluation, incident commanders can ensure that resources are optimally utilized, tactical objectives are met, and the safety of occupants and response personnel is assured. By following NFPA, ICAO, FAA regulations, and the principles set forth in IFSTA's *Aircraft Rescue and Fire Fighting* book, Aircraft Rescue Firefighters can conduct accurate and effective assessments that contribute to successful operations and continuous improvement of emergency response practices.

In addition, the assessment allows for a more efficient use of resources, ensuring that response teams operate in a safe and coordinated manner, following international NFPA, ICAO and FAA regulations. Implementing a rigorous and systematic assessment during an incident is key to the success of any emergency response operation.

Assessing progress in an aviation emergency is a complex process that requires the use of advanced tools and well-defined methods. Key performance indicators (KPIs) provide a quantitative basis for measuring the success of operations, while the use of real-time monitoring technology allows response teams to obtain an accurate and up-to-date view of the incident. By following NFPA, ICAO, and FAA regulations, and using emergency management best practices, incident commanders can ensure continuous and effective evaluation, which contributes to the overall success of the aircraft rescue and fire suppression operation.

Personnel performance evaluation is a critical component of aviation emergency management, identifying both individual and team performance, ensuring that the objectives of the IAP are met safely and effectively. By following NFPA, ICAO, and FAA regulations, incident commanders can assess the technical and tactical capability of response personnel, monitor their safety, and ensure that the risks inherent in rescue and fire suppression operations are minimized. Implementing rigorous and continuous assessments not only improves operational effectiveness, but also ensures the safety and well-being of Aircraft Rescue Firefighters.

Assessing resource effectiveness is a vital part of aviation emergency management. Through analysis of the proper use of equipment and materials, water and foam supply capabilities, and the effectiveness of resupply methods, incident commanders can ensure that resources are optimally utilized to achieve the objectives of the Incident Action Plan. By following NFPA, ICAO and FAA regulations, and utilizing emergency management best practices, aeronautical fire crews can continually improve the effectiveness of their operations, ensuring a faster and safer response in future emergencies.

Review and adjustment of the Incident Action Plan is an ongoing and critical task during any aviation emergency. Real-time feedback, combined with clear procedures for making adjustments, ensures that responders can adapt to the dynamic conditions of an incident. Real-life cases of adaptation demonstrate how quick and effective adjustments can be critical to the success of a rescue and firefighting operation. By following NFPA, ICAO, FAA and other international organizations, incident commanders can ensure that the AIP remains a flexible and effective tool for dealing with complex emergencies.

Proper document management and progress reporting is an integral part of continuous assessment during aviation emergencies. Assessment records and interim reports allow incident commanders to make decisions based on accurate and up-to-date information, improve coordination between response teams and ensure efficiency in the use of resources. In addition, this documentation is critical for post-incident analysis, facilitating the continuous improvement of operating procedures and the development of more effective tactics for future emergencies.

Measuring impact and outcome is a critical part of evaluating the effectiveness of aeronautical emergency operations. Comparing the results obtained with the objectives set at the beginning of the incident provides valuable information to improve future procedures, while analyzing the impact on infrastructure and the environment ensures that operations do not cause unnecessary long-term damage. By following NFPA, ICAO and FAA regulations, incident commanders and fire crews can conduct comprehensive assessments that continually improve emergency response capabilities.

## TACTICS AND STRATEGIES FOR AIRCRAFT FIREFIGHTING

## References

FAA (2020). *Aircraft rescue and firefighting plan (Advisory Circular 150/5210-17C)*. Federal Aviation Administration.

IFSTA (2020). *Aircraft Rescue and Fire Fighting*. International Fire Service Training Association.

ICAO. (2019). *Airport Services Manual - Part 1: Rescue and Firefighting*. International Civil Aviation Organization.

NFPA. (2022). *NFPA 403: Standard for Aircraft Rescue and Fire-Fighting Services at Airports*. National Fire Protection Association.

NFPA. (2022). *NFPA 1561: Standard on Emergency Services Incident Management System and Command Safety*. National Fire Protection Association.

*NFPA. (2022).* NFPA 1500: Standard on Fire Department Occupational Safety, Health, and Wellness Program. *National Fire Protection Association.*

NTSB. (2014). *Asiana Airlines Flight 214 Accident Report*.

# CHAPTER 5

# ENDING THE INCIDENT

# TACTICS AND STRATEGIES FOR AIRCRAFT FIREFIGHTING

## INTRODUCTION

The conclusion of an emergency operation is as crucial as its beginning. At this point in the process, the decisions made, and actions taken can have a significant impact on the safety of equipment, the overall effectiveness of the response, and the resilience of the affected environment. **Chapter 5: Ending the Incident** focuses on the steps necessary to formally close operations of an aeronautical incident, covering aspects such as **demobilization, operational closure, administrative closure,** and **post-incident review.**

Ending an incident involves much more than simply withdrawing resources; it requires a methodical approach to ensure that all risks have been mitigated, operations have been properly documented, and lessons learned are integrated to improve future responses. The *National Fire Protection Association* (NFPA), *International Civil Aviation Organization (ICAO),* and *Federal Aviation Administration* (FAA) regulations provide a clear structure to guide these processes, ensuring that safety protocols are followed, and residual risks are minimized.

One of the key elements at the end of an incident is the **Post Incident Meeting (PIM)** or *critique*, which provides a space for all stakeholders to reflect on what happened and provide feedback on performance and tactics employed. These meetings allow teams to identify both successes and areas for improvement, helping to refine future procedures. According to **FEMA** guidelines, a proper PRI and detailed debriefing allows for continuous learning, strengthening operational capability to deal with new emergencies.

This chapter also addresses **demobilization** processes, in which resources and personnel are safely and orderly removed from the incident site. In addition, **administrative closure** and the importance of **proper documentation** to ensure accountability and facilitate post-incident review are covered. Finally, the chapter focuses on creating **improvement plans** based on lessons learned to ensure better preparedness and response in future aviation emergencies.

The primary objective of this chapter is to provide a comprehensive guide to enable emergency leaders to effectively end an incident, ensuring that every aspect of the process is evaluated, documented and improved.

# TACTICS AND STRATEGIES FOR AIRCRAFT FIREFIGHTING

## 5.1 Debriefing or after-action review

The Debriefing should be done in the heat of the moment, it is an informal meeting that allows us to close the cycle, if there was a briefing there should be a debriefing, do not miss the opportunity to thank people for their delivery, remember that we are emotional beings and that we always require recognition, although we do not do it with that objective, unconsciously we need it.

It also offers the personnel who worked on the incident the opportunity to "replay" the event, extract lessons learned and evaluate performance, focus on the elements of communication and teamwork (managers and subordinates), evaluate critical decisions made and reinforce the importance of situational awareness.

IMPORTANT: Identify the need for Psychological Intervention, evaluate the emotions and coping capacity of the responders to the events that have just occurred, take advantage of the space to initiate psychological ventilation, if someone requires more time, or is noticeably affected, activate the mental health route so that a professional with training in emergency psychology is in charge.

## Components

- Who responded?
- What did they do?
- When did they?
- How effective was your operation?

## Key issues

- Health information
- Equipment exhibition
- Contact person for follow-up.

- Identified problems requiring immediate action.
- Say THANK YOU

**When?**

- Must begin as soon as the emergency phase is over.
- Before anyone leaves the scene

**Procedure**

- Distractions-free area
- Driven by a single person (IC may not be the best person)
- Maximum 15 minutes
- Collect information.
- Not a CRITIQUE

### 5.2 Operational Closing

Operational closure is the process by which all tactical and logistical activities associated with the response to an aeronautical fire are formally concluded. This process involves verification that the objectives of the Incident Action Plan (IAP) have been met and that the scene is safe for normal airport operations to resume. Operational closure also encompasses the orderly removal of equipment, assessment of the final situation and coordination with other involved institutions to ensure that no residual risks remain.

The closure of an operation requires a series of steps to ensure that the incident has been fully controlled, risks have been mitigated, and all resources have been effectively managed. This process is a direct reflection of the effectiveness of the Incident Action Plan and the ability of aeronautical fire crews to respond to emergencies quickly and safely. The National Fire Protection Association (NFPA), the International Civil Aviation Organization (ICAO), and the Federal

Aviation Administration (FAA) establish specific guidelines to ensure that operational shutdown is conducted to the highest safety standards (NFPA 1561, 2022; ICAO, 2019).

### 5.2.1 Demobilization

Demobilization is an essential part of operational closure, as it involves the orderly withdrawal of resources and personnel deployed during the emergency. This process must be carried out in a coordinated manner, to avoid leaving gaps in safety and to ensure that all equipment is returned to normal operational status. According to NFPA 1561, demobilization should be planned in advance as part of the IAP, and should include clear steps to ensure that critical resources are not removed until it has been verified that the incident has been fully controlled (NFPA 1561, 2022), this orderly process is performed on SCI Form 221.

### Steps for Demobilization

1. **Incident Status Assessment:** Prior to commencing demobilization, the Incident commander should conduct a thorough assessment of the situation to ensure that no active hotspots of risk remain. This includes verifying that all fires have been completely extinguished, that there is no risk of re-ignition, and that the aircraft has been secured. The FAA recommends that all affected areas, including cargo compartments and aircraft electrical systems, be carefully checked (FAA, 2020).

2. **Removal of resources in a phased manner:** The removal of resources should be done in a phased manner, starting with non-essential equipment and leaving critical resources in place until complete safety is assured. Aeronautical fire equipment should be removed in an orderly manner, with accurate records of each unit and piece of equipment being demobilized. NFPA 1500 states that demobilization should be documented and coordinated among all teams involved to avoid confusion or errors (NFPA 1500, 2022).

3. **Restoration of resources and equipment:** As resources are removed, it is critical to restore them to operational status for future emergencies. This includes resupplying firefighting equipment, inspecting fire vehicles, and repairing any equipment that was damaged during the incident. The Incident Command System (ICS), described by FEMA, stresses the importance of preparedness for the next incident, which involves the immediate implementation of restoration and maintenance processes (FEMA, 2017).

4. **Coordination with other institutions:** Demobilization is not limited only to Aircraft Rescue Firefighters. It is essential to coordinate the process with other institutions involved, such as airport authorities, security forces and medical services. ICAO recommends constant communication between all parties to ensure that the airport can resume operations safely and efficiently once demobilization is completed (ICAO, 2019).

**Key Considerations**

Demobilization should be viewed not only as the end of one operation, but as preparation for the next. During this process, operation leaders should consider the following:

- **Personnel safety:** Removal of equipment and personnel must be done in a safe manner, without rushing and ensuring that all risks have been eliminated before the resources are removed.

- **Restoration of airport infrastructure:** It is important to assess whether airport infrastructure, such as runways and hangars, has been damaged during operation and to coordinate with the authorities to make the necessary repairs.

- **Complete documentation:** The entire demobilization process should be properly documented. NFPA and FEMA stress the need for detailed record keeping, including actions taken during the incident, resources used, and lessons learned, to ensure that improvements can be implemented in future responses (NFPA 1561, 2022; FEMA, 2017).

## 5.3 Administrative Closing

The **administrative closure** of an aeronautical emergency is a crucial part of the incident management process. This process involves the collection, analysis and documentation of all relevant information related to the operation, including records of resources used, actions taken during the incident, and the results obtained. Administrative closure not only serves the function of formalizing the end of the incident, but also provides a documentary basis that can be used for audits, performance evaluations and lessons learned.

According to the *National Fire Protection Association* (NFPA), the *International Civil Aviation Organization (ICAO)*, and the *Federal Aviation Administration* (FAA), aeronautical incident documentation should include a comprehensive report detailing all aspects of the event, from initial mobilization to final demobilization of resources. Administrative closure should also involve a structured review of the incident to identify areas for improvement. This process also includes post-incident review meetings, known as **Post-Incident Meetings (PIMs)** or *critiques*, which are intended to improve future response capability.

### 5.3.1 Post Incident Meeting (PIM) or Critique

The **Post Incident Meeting (PIM)** or *critique* is a critical component of administrative closure. It is a systematic review of the actions and decisions made during the incident response. The purpose of this meeting is to provide an environment where participants can share their experiences, identify what worked well and point out areas for improvement.

According to *FEMA* regulations and *NFPA 1561*, PRI has several key objectives:

- **Evaluate tactical and operational performance**: Review whether the tactics employed during the incident were effective and whether available resources were used appropriately.
- **Identify lessons learned**: Document what worked and what did not, so that these lessons can be applied to improve preparedness and response in future incidents.
- **Strengthen interagency coordination**: In aviation emergencies, operations often involve multiple institutions. PRI provides an opportunity to assess coordination between these institutions and improve inter-organizational relationships.

### 5.3.1.1 Immediate Post-Incident Meeting (RPII)

The **Immediate Post Incident Debriefing (IIBD)** is a preliminary version of the formal IPR that takes place immediately after the incident. Its purpose is to gather initial impressions and real-time reactions from the response teams while the details of the event are still fresh in the minds of the participants.

The RPII should be conducted within 24 to 48 hours of the incident, allowing operational leaders to gain a clear picture of field operations. This meeting focuses on tactical aspects and personnel safety. According to *FEMA* guidelines, the RPII should be brief, focused, and should include a quick review of response procedures and personnel safety (FEMA, 2017).

### 5.3.1.2 Formal Post-Incident Meeting (Formal PIM)

The **Formal Post Incident Meeting** is a more detailed and structured assessment that takes place days or weeks after the incident, once all reports and records have been compiled. This meeting includes all key players, from the Incident commander to team leaders, and is intended to evaluate all aspects of the incident in depth.

According to *NFPA 1561*, formal PRI should address both achievements and areas for improvement, providing a more complete view of operational effectiveness. In addition, it focuses on:

- **Review of resources used**: A detailed analysis is made of the resources deployed, such as vehicles, equipment, extinguishing agents, and personnel, to determine whether they were used efficiently.
- **Staff safety discussion**: The safety procedures followed during the incident are evaluated, identifying any failures or areas for improvement to ensure staff protection in future responses.
- **Development of improvement plans**: Based on the findings of the RPI, a continuous improvement plan should be developed that includes clear recommendations for training and updating of operating procedures (NFPA 1561, 2022).

### 5.4 Final Report

The **Final Report** is one of the most important parts of the management process of an aeronautical incident, as it provides a detailed analysis of all aspects of the event, from the moment it occurred until the closure of operations. This document serves as a formal record of the actions taken, resources used, and results achieved during the incident, and becomes a reference for improving future responses. Guidelines from the *National Fire Protection Association* (NFPA), the *International Civil Aviation Organization (ICAO)*, the *Federal Aviation Administration* (FAA), and agencies such as *FEMA* and *USAID BHA*, stress the importance of a well-structured report, including an executive summary, lessons learned, and a complete analysis of the operations.

## TACTICS AND STRATEGIES FOR AIRCRAFT FIREFIGHTING

### 5.4.1 Executive Summary

The **Executive Summary** is a high-level synthesis of the final report that provides an overview of the actions taken and the results achieved. Its purpose is to provide decision-makers and other interested parties with a clear and concise understanding of the incident, without the need to review the entire report in detail.

**The summary should address key issues such as:**

- **Description of the incident**: A brief description of what happened, including the type of aircraft, the location of the incident, and the circumstances leading to the emergency.
- **Response Actions**: A summary of key actions taken by aeronautical fire crews, including Incident Action Plan (IAP) activation, fire suppression methods used, and evacuation tactics.
- **Results**: A summary of the results obtained, such as complete fire suppression, the number of people rescued, and the overall safety of response personnel and aircraft occupants.

The executive summary should be clear, concise, and contain sufficient information for decision makers to evaluate the effectiveness of the response. According to *FEMA* guidelines, this section should also highlight the challenges faced and how they were overcome, providing a balanced focus on the positive aspects and those requiring improvement (FEMA, 2017).

### 5.4.2 Lessons Learned

The **lessons learned** analysis is a critical part of the final report, as it provides a space to document what worked well during the incident and what did not. Lessons learned should be practical and actionable, with the goal of improving future response capabilities.

## TACTICS AND STRATEGIES FOR AIRCRAFT FIREFIGHTING

**Key areas to review in this section include:**

- **Tactics employed**: Evaluate firefighting, rescue tactics, and determine if they were effective. For example, whether AFFF foam was used correctly and in adequate quantities, or if there were problems with the deployment of extinguishing equipment.
- **Interagency coordination**: In many aeronautical incidents, the response involves the collaboration of multiple institutions. Lessons learned should assess whether coordination between these institutions was effective and how it could be improved in future emergencies. *NFPA 1561* stresses the importance of identifying communication problems that could have occurred during the response (NFPA 1561, 2022).
- **Resource management**: It is important to assess whether the resources available during the incident, such as extinguishing vehicles, personal protective equipment, and extinguishing agents, were sufficient and used effectively. *ICAO* recommends that airports document any deficiencies in resource availability or resupply logistics (ICAO, 2019).

Lessons learned should be incorporated into future training plans, and shared with other airports or institutions that may face similar incidents. This process ensures that best practices are widely disseminated, and adjustments are made where necessary.

### 5.4.3 Reference Material

**Reference material** provides operational managers and future responders with access to key documents used during the incident, as well as the protocols and regulations followed. Materials that should be included in this section include:

- **Incident Action Plans (IAPs)**: The IAPs used during the operation, including established objectives and designed tactics, should be kept on file for future reference.
- **Regulations and operational guidelines**: Regulatory documents from *NFPA*, *ICAO*, *FAA*, and other organizations, which were used as a basis for decision making during the incident.
- **Technical reports and safety assessments**: Any assessment made before, during or after the incident that influenced the decisions made.

This material serves not only as a historical archive, but also as a learning tool for future incidents, ensuring that the knowledge gained during the event can be applied to other similar scenarios (FEMA, 2017).

### 5.4.4 Sample Final Report

The **final report template** is a standardized format that facilitates the clear and structured presentation of all information related to the incident. This template can be adapted according to the needs of each airport or agency, but should follow a logical structure covering all phases of the incident, from IAP activation to demobilization and administrative closure.

**The report template should include the following sections:**

- **Introduction**: A general description of the incident, including the context, the circumstances leading to the emergency, and the objectives of the EPI.
- **Actions taken**: A detailed analysis of the tactical actions taken by the response teams, from initial arrival at the incident site to the final suppression of the fire and evacuation of the victims.

- **Performance evaluation**: A review of the operational performance of the teams, focusing on the effectiveness of tactics employed and resources used.

- **Results**: A summary of the results obtained, including lives saved, fire containment and impact on airport infrastructure.

- **Conclusions and recommendations**: This section should include both lessons learned and recommendations for improving response capabilities in the future.

This standardized format ensures that all relevant information is documented in an organized and understandable manner, facilitating its use in future training and emergency planning operations (NFPA 1561, 2022).

### 5.5 Post Lessons Learned Analysis Improvement Plans

Once the lessons learned from an aircraft incident has been completed, it is critical to develop **improvement plans** based on the findings identified during the After-Action Review (AAR) and Post Incident Meeting (PIM). This process ensures that lessons learned from the incident are translated into concrete actions to improve responsiveness to future events, strengthen operational safety and avoid repetition of errors.

Improvement plans are a key tool in emergency management, providing a structured framework for implementing change, ensuring that best practices are effectively adopted, and fostering a cycle of continuous improvement in response operations. According to the *National Fire Protection Association* (NFPA), *International Civil Aviation Organization (ICAO), Federal Aviation Administration* (FAA), and agencies such as *FEMA* and *USAID BHA*, improvement plans should include clear goals, defined timelines and assignment of responsibilities to ensure their successful execution.

## 5.5.1 Development of Improvement Plans

The development of an improvement plan should be a collaborative process that involves all stakeholders in the incident response, from the Incident commander to the leaders of the operational teams and representatives of the institutions involved. According to *FEMA*, it is essential that the plan be based on objective data and detailed analysis drawn from the AAR, which ensures that decisions are grounded in hard evidence (FEMA, 2017).

Steps for developing an effective improvement plan include:

1. **Identification of key areas for improvement**: The first step is to prioritize the areas for improvement identified in the AAR, whether in terms of operational tactics, interagency coordination, resource management or personnel safety. *NFPA 1561* recommends focusing on those areas that have the greatest impact on the safety and efficiency of operations (NFPA 1561, 2022).

2. **SMART goal setting**: Goals should be specific, measurable, achievable, realistic and time-bound (*SMART*). This allows progress to be clearly assessed and facilitates accountability. For example, if a gap in coordination between institutions was identified, a SMART goal could be "Improve interoperability between aeronautical fire teams and LCA medical services by implementing a common communications system within the next three months" (ICAO, 2019).

3. **Assignment of responsibilities**: Each action within the improvement plan should have a designated responsible party, who will be in charge of implementing the necessary actions and monitoring their progress. It is important that these responsibilities are assigned at appropriate levels within the operational structure, ensuring that team leaders and resource persons have the authority to implement the required changes (USAID BHA, 2021).

4. **Establishment of timelines**: The plan should include a clear timeline for implementing the improvements. The timelines should be realistic, but urgent enough to ensure that changes are made before another similar incident occurs. This should also include dates for interim assessments, where progress is reviewed and strategies adjusted if necessary (FEMA, 2017).

### 5.5.2 Common Areas for Improvement

From the analysis of past aeronautical incidents, the following common areas often require improvement plans:

1. **Inter-agency coordination**: Aeronautical emergency response often involves multiple institutions, from firefighters to medical services, security forces and airport operators. Failures in communication and coordination between these institutions can delay operations and jeopardize the safety of personnel and passengers. An improvement plan should address how to improve interoperability through joint drills, interagency training, and the use of interoperable communication systems (NFPA 1500, 2022).

2. **Personnel training**: Many of the lessons learned often reveal areas where response personnel need more training. This may include the use of new equipment, the application of more effective fire suppression tactics, or improved aircraft evacuation procedures. Improvement plans should include training programs focused on strengthening these skills (ICAO, 2019).

3. **Resource management and logistics**: In some cases, emergency responses may be hampered by a lack of critical resources or logistical problems, such as insufficient AFFF foam or poor distribution of equipment. Improvement plans should address how to ensure continued availability of needed resources and improve resupply systems (FAA, 2020).

## 5.5.3 Improvement Plan Monitoring and Evaluation

Once the improvement plan is implemented, it is critical to perform continuous monitoring to ensure that the proposed actions are achieving the desired results. According to *FEMA* guidelines, this includes conducting periodic evaluations and drills to measure the effectiveness of improvements and adjust actions as needed (FEMA, 2017).

Follow-up should include collecting data and conducting interviews or surveys of personnel involved in the response to assess whether improvements have had a positive impact. If new areas for improvement are identified during follow-up, they should be integrated into the continuous improvement plan.

## Conclusion

Debriefing or After-Action Review (AAR) is a critical tool to ensure that every incident becomes an opportunity for continuous hot learning and improvement. Through rapid, focused analysis of lessons learned, aeronautical fire crews can improve their tactics and procedures, ensuring a more effective and safer response in future emergencies. NFPA, FEMA and FAA regulations clearly state the importance of this process to enhance operational readiness and safety in aeronautical firefighting operations.

The debriefing should focus on identifying with the responders their emotional state and coping with the events that occurred, verify the need for structured or unstructured intervention with a mental health professional, review compliance with objectives, quickly identify opportunities for improvement, close the operations cycle, if there is a field briefing the most logical thing to do is to have a debriefing, do not skip this important opportunity to conclude the operational phase.

Operational shutdown and demobilization are critical phases in the management of an aeronautical fire incident. Ensuring that these processes are conducted in an orderly, safe, and efficient manner is critical to ensure full recovery of the airport and prepare teams for future emergencies. NFPA, ICAO, FAA, and FEMA regulations provide clear guidelines for conducting these processes effectively, ensuring that resources are ready for reuse and that lessons learned are documented and integrated into future planning.

Administrative closure is a critical phase of the emergency management cycle in which all relevant incident information is collected and analyzed, and the end of operations is formalized. Through Post Incident Meetings (PIM), both immediate and formal, the organizations involved can identify strengths and weaknesses, and apply lessons learned to improve their preparedness and future response. Following NFPA, FEMA, ICAO, and FAA regulations, administrative closure should be a structured process that ensures continuous improvement and organizational learning.

Lessons learned post analysis improvement plans are an essential tool to ensure that emergency response organizations can adapt and continually improve. Following *NFPA*, *ICAO*, *FAA*, and *FEMA* regulations, these plans provide a clear roadmap for implementing changes, ensuring personnel safety, and improving responsiveness to future aviation incidents. The creation and effective execution of these plans ensures that every incident becomes an opportunity to learn and strengthen operations.

Scan the QR code to view the book's conclusions

# TACTICS AND STRATEGIES FOR AIRCRAFT FIREFIGHTING

## References

FAA (2020). *Aircraft rescue and firefighting plan (Advisory Circular 150/5210-17C)*. Federal Aviation Administration.

IFSTA (2020). *Aircraft Rescue and Fire Fighting*. International Fire Service Training Association.

ICAO. (2019). *Airport Services Manual - Part 1: Rescue and Firefighting*. International Civil Aviation Organization.

NFPA. (2022). *NFPA 403: Standard for Aircraft Rescue and Fire-Fighting Services at Airports*. National Fire Protection Association.

NFPA. (2022). *NFPA 1500: Standard on Fire Department Occupational Safety, Health, and Wellness Program*. National Fire Protection Association.

NFPA. (2022). *NFPA 1561: Standard on Emergency Services Incident Management System and Command Safety*. National Fire Protection Association.

USAID BHA (2021). Incident Command System Operations Manual.

FEMA (2017). *Incident Command System for Emergency Response (IS-200)*. Federal Emergency Management Agency.

NTSB. (2014). *Asiana Airlines Flight 214 Accident Report*. National Transportation Safety Board.

# ACKNOWLEDGMENTS

My first thanks will always be to my wife Lorena, you are the source of inspiration for everything I do, my engine, my light, everything I want to undertake has an echo in you and I receive unconditional support.

To my children Juan Felipe and Juliana for your support, for motivating me to be a better person, because without your life would not have the meaning it has today.

To my father, my mother, my siblings and my entire family, thank you for your constant support, and thank you for teaching me that family is the most important thing, now that family is complete.

To my in-laws for their support and constant encouragement when I falter.

To my coworkers for always being attentive and celebrating my triumphs, for supporting me throughout all these years and helping me to implement everything we could do to guarantee a professional Fire and Rescue Service at the service of aviation.

To the Civil Aeronautics of Colombia, for being my home throughout these almost 26 years.

# TACTICS AND STRATEGIES FOR AIRCRAFT FIREFIGHTING

Made in United States
Orlando, FL
09 December 2024

55266676R00117